HISTORIC BRISTOL

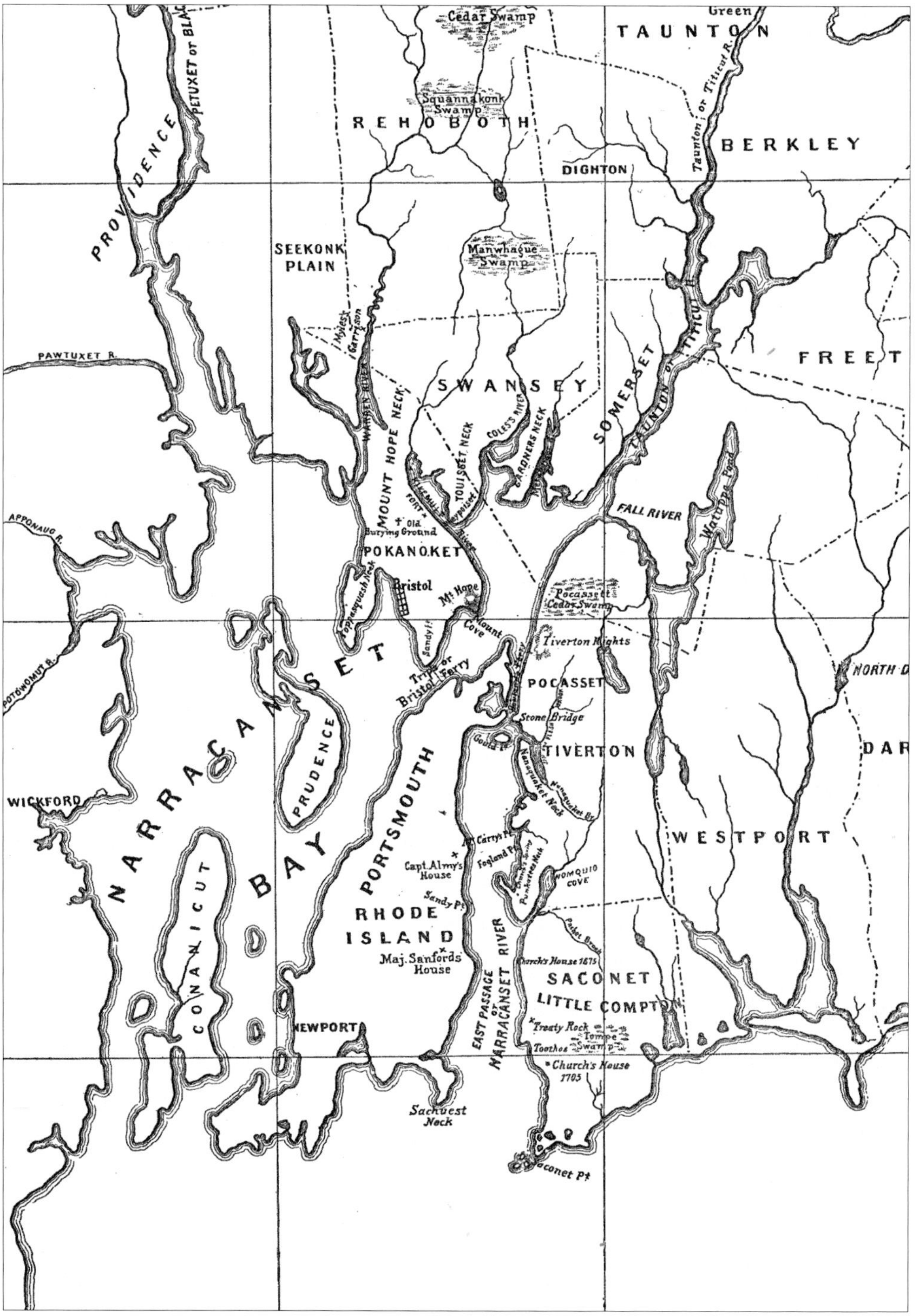

King Philip's country.

HISTORIC BRISTOL

TALES FROM AN OLD RHODE ISLAND SEAPORT

RICHARD V. SIMPSON

THE History PRESS

Published by The History Press
Charleston, SC 29403
www.historypress.net

Cover image: *Rainbow* and *White Hawk II* at the Herreshoff Marine Museum dock in Bristol. *Photo by Bonnie Blue, courtesy of the Herreshoff Marine Museum/America's Cup Hall of Fame, www.herreshoff.org.*

First published 2008

Manufactured in the United States

ISBN 978.1.59629.352.6

Library of Congress Cataloging-in-Publication Data

Simpson, Richard V.
Historic Bristol : tales from an old Rhode Island seaport / Richard V. Simpson.
p. cm.
Includes bibliographical references.
ISBN-13: 978-1-59629-352-6 (alk. paper)
1. Bristol (R.I.)--History--Anecdotes. I. Title.
F89.B8S57 2007
974.5'5--dc22
2007042252

Contents

Preface	Historic Mount Hope	7
Acknowledgements		9
Introduction	The Vikings and Mount Hope	11
Chapter One	Montaup and Metacomet	19
Chapter Two	Settlement	25
Chapter Three	Point Pleasant Farm	31
Chapter Four	Poppasquash Neck, Redcrest and the Bristol Yacht Club	37
Chapter Five	Commerce	43
Chapter Six	A Summary of Public Education for Two Centuries	55
Chapter Seven	Federal-era Architect Russell Warren	71
Chapter Eight	Mr. Anthony Quinn's Bristol Performance	79
Chapter Nine	Rights-of-Way to the Water	83
Chapter Ten	The New Look	91
Chapter Eleven	More Tales from an Old Seaport	119
Chapter Twelve	Gleanings from a Century of the *Bristol Phoenix*	145
Notes		153
Bibliography		155
About the Author		157

An allegorical view of Mount Hope from the west.

PREFACE

HISTORIC MOUNT HOPE

The town of Bristol is most fortunate in having a promontory so eminent as Mount Hope Neck and an eminence of such historical prominence as Mount Hope. Shadowy tradition and authentic history conspire to make Bristol's mountain, in height scarcely two hundred feet above the waters of Mount Hope Bay, quite as celebrated as the more aspiring peaks of classic lands across the sea. The very name is so antique in origin that no scholar of the Indian tongue has been able to tell us whether the Norse navigators of 1000 A.D. first inscribed "Hop" on the cliffs above a land-locked sea. Or the great tribe that once reveled on its rocky summit called it Montaup or the early English of the time of the Cabots or of John Smith named it Mount Hope, as the land they had long desired to see. From whatever tongue or time the name Mount Hope has come, it has come to stay and Bristol will ever hold sacred the possession of the ancestral, pre-colonial name.

Anonymous Author
Bristol Phoenix Industrial Edition, 1903

Acknowledgements

Thanks to *Bristol Phoenix* editor Ted Hayes for allowing use of *Phoenix* photos and graphics; also thanks to *Bristol Phoenix* publisher Matthew Hayes for allowing use of the Colonel Colt's Mercedes, and the General Ambrose E. Burnside and Private Edward Anthony Jr. articles.

I am indebted to the Newport Collaborative Architects for supplying the Thames Street Landing and Belvedere Hotel images.

Sincere thanks to Bristol Town Clerk Louis Cirillo, who aided in qualifying some of the most salient details in this volume.

The author has endeavored to identify the sources of the photographs, illustrations and narrative passages; generally, sources are in the public domain. Unless otherwise noted, all images are from the author's collection.

Introduction

The Vikings and Mount Hope

Any Rhode Islander with even a casual interest in the history of this state is advised to find a copy of J. Earl Clauson's *These Plantations*, a slim volume published in 1937 by the Roger Williams Press. In the book's first chapter, "The Vikings," Clauson offers conclusive proof of a Norwegian settlement on the shores of Mount Hope, from AD 1000 to 1003.

According to Clauson:

> *When William B. Goodwin of Hartford excavated Fort Ninigret in Charleston, Rhode Island he buttressed his thesis that the site of the fort was originally a Dutch trading post. This thesis was presented in a lecture before the Rhode Island Historical Society on the place called Norembega.*
>
> *Norembega City is a more or less mythical spot taking its name from Norawegia or something corrupted to that spelling by people who didn't care how they spelled. Goodwin located Norembega City as a trading post at the junction of the Hudson and Mohawk Rivers. A deed found in the British Records Office shows that Sir Charles Peckham and son were granted a tract of one million and half acres west from Narragansett Bay, at the time referred to as the Dee River, for services rendered to Sir Humphrey Gilbert.*
>
> *By this, Goodwin presents a reasonably strong case that Norembega was Rhode Island and the land westward to a point beyond the Connecticut. Since the name is presumably a hang-over from Viking establishment in the new world, locating the place helps to circumscribe a little the inquiry as to where it was the Ericsson boys and their comrades landed.*

Clauson, an archaeologist, says that at the time of his writing he was in possession of a battle axe that was dug up in 1889 on the site of the Saunders House at Saunderstown, Rhode Island.

A Viking long keelboat.

> *From the known facts we advance modestly, without fear of successful refutation, the theory that Leif Ericsson's settlement, known to us archaeologists as Leif's Booths, was either at Saunderstown or a bit south of there.*
>
> *You may think what you like about it* [the battle axe]*; we claim it has been lying there since the Vikings had a fight with the Indians on that strand about 1003 A.D.*
>
> *Leif Ericsson and his crew put out from the settlement in Greenland in 1000. After being pushed along for several days and nights by a stiff nor'easter, they found refuge in a still backwater where a river drops into the ocean from a lake. There they built huts, passed the winter and, because of the abundance of grapes, named the place Vinland.*
>
> *Various scholars, chiefly Norwegian, have identified Vinland with Mount Hope Bay. They point out that the entrance suggests a river flowing from a lake, and say also that "Hop" is an Old Norse word for lake and that Montaup, the Wampanoag name for the place, derived from the word the Vikings applied to it.* [W.H. Munro suggests Hop probably was the origin of the Indian name Haup or Montaup, from which the present name Mount Hope is derived.]
>
> *Arguments in support of the idea that Leif wintered on the shore of Mount Hope Bay are of the sort that you can take or leave alone. There are two inscribed rocks, Dighton and another on the Bristol shore, which Scandinavian scholars claim are Runic. The conclusions of Professor E.B. Delabarre, of Brown, are that the markings on Dighton, instead of being Runic, were made by Indians except for the name Miguel Cortereal and the date 1511. These he believes were carved by a Portuguese navigator, who became leader of the Indians thereabouts.*
>
> *There are two other bits of alleged evidence. One was the skeleton in armor dug up at Fall River* [Massachusetts]*, which Longfellow wrote a poem about. The second is another skeleton in armor dug up on Gardner's Neck, Swansea.*
>
> *Professor Delabarre believes both of these were Indian skeletons. Their so-called armor was of copper, obtained by trading with western tribes. The Scandinavian scholars think they were Viking remains. Howard Gardner of Gardner's Neck* [Connecticut]*, who has maintained a lifetime interest in Indian relics, says the armor was of brass, not copper, and where in the world would the Indians get brass?*

Scandinavian sagas tell of the voyages south to the land called Vin. The sagas establish the fact that the Vikings came into Narragansett Bay and landed on the shores of Mount Hope. Thorfinn Karlsefni, a Norse seaman, raised a colony of 151 men and 7 women, left Greenland in 1007 and sailed to mild and pleasant Vinland. They found the houses built by Leif Ericsson in AD 1000. They erected more and organized a colony. At first they lived in peace with the natives (Skraelings, or "lean men," the Norse called them). The colonists were eventually driven from the land by the natives, probably for too enthusiastically encroaching upon them. So they returned to Greenland in 1010.

Though Karlsefni did not succeed in colonizing the country, other Norsemen probably came and lived here. This is assumed because records show an order commanding the Bishop of Greenland to make a trip to Vinland in 1121; this seems to prove there must have been remnants from the established Viking colony in the territory. However, all records of the colonists were eventually lost and so their existence is merely a matter of conjecture.

It is pleasant to believe that the very name Mount Hope has come down from these Icelanders, having been incorporated into the language of the Indians in the vicinity and passed onto the first English settlers at Plymouth. Otherwise little trace remains of the visits of these first explorers, unless the queer inscriptions on the rock at the shore in Bristol's Hopeworth area, north of the foot of Mount Hope, are thought to be the work of their hands. Sadly, the stone, although still extant, washed by the ocean for so many centuries, has deteriorated severely. Biarni, Leif Ericsson, Thorvald and Thorfinn—these were the prominent Viking leaders who came here and attempted to establish settlements. It is thought the last of the Norsemen had returned to Iceland and Scandinavia after the visit of the Bishop of Greenland in 1121.

Native Names for Rhode Island Places

Rhode Island is rich in names of places and expressions derived and modified from native origins. Some have changed little, or not at all, from the original forms interpreted and written down by the white foreigner: Yawgoog, Woonsocket, Pawtucket, Narragansett, Quequatucket, Apponaug, Natick, Shannock, Weybosset and Woonasquatucket are some of the common and familiar place names. Besides these, there are many sites in Rhode Island that owe the origin of their names to incidents of more or less importance in local native history and legend, for example: Carbuncle Pond, Nine Men's Misery, Coronation Rock, Church Cove, Drum Rock Hill, Indian Run and Queen River. But, except for the names of certain tribes and a few important chieftains, the term most closely associated with Native American history in southern New England is Mount Hope, the name given to the hill and surrounding lands located a short distance east of the business center of Bristol, Rhode Island.

More than one theory exists concerning the origin of the name Mount Hope, given to the place originally referred to by the natives as Pokanoket. The Wampanoag people who still live in Bristol refer to their clan as the Pokanoket tribe. It is also reasonable to conclude that the name is a corruption of the natives' name for the place—Montaup. We may assume, therefore, that the Indians at one time or another referred to this hill with gently sloping sides by a name that sounded, when spoken, something like that which the white man finally wrote down as Mount Hope. It has been variously spelled from the earliest days as Montaup, Mountup or Mont-haup. It is quite possible that the name may have been a corruption or simplification of the last two syllables of the Indian word

Uppaquontup, meaning "the head." It can be easily observed how that particular descriptive term might have been applied to such a dominating land feature.

Regardless of whether the natives replaced the ancient name of Pokanoket with something that apparently had the sound of a simple combination of two common English words, or whether the white man, possibly Roger Williams, renamed the spot with its present designation just as he named his settlement Providence and three Narragansett Bay islands Prudence, Patience and Hope, the fact remains that Mount Hope was one of the very first names to be applied to any place in North America by both Europeans and by the first white men who settled on these shores. Likewise, Mount Hope has always been and, doubtless, will remain forever a place of great historical significance, principally because of its intimate association with one of the leading figures in the first century of American history.

The Native People

Almost six hundred years after the Vikings, in 1620, when the first English pilgrims placed their feet on Cape Cod sand, the Mount Hope Lands were under the rule of Massasoit, the statesman-like leader of the Wampanoag Nation.

In the early seventeenth century, the land surrounding Narragansett Bay was divided between two rival Native American tribes: the Narragansett on the west shore and the Wampanoag on the east shore. Both tribes belonged to the Algonquin language group, and they followed a pattern of seasonal migration between coastal fields and inland hunting and fishing areas.

Massasoit, great sachem of the Wampanoag, controlled the land reaching from Narragansett Bay east to Massachusetts Bay. His headquarters were in what is now Bristol, known to the colonists as the Mount Hope Lands. His tribal councils were held in eastern Bristol in the shelter of a cliff at Mount Hope. A Wampanoag village was located at Pokanoket in Bristol on the northeast shore of Mount Hope Bay, an area now called the Narrows.

Throughout the mid-seventeenth century, three colonies of European settlers were expanding into Massasoit's lands; each was to play a role in Bristol's first century. In 1620, Plymouth Colony on Cape Cod was settled by separatists who were dissatisfied with the established church in England. Massachusetts Bay Colony was settled in 1629 by people who, like those at Plymouth, were dissatisfied with the English church. Emigrants from these two older colonies also settled in the area that is now Rhode Island, seeking to escape the religious conformity of the separatist colonies. Roger Williams settled in Providence in 1636; Anne Hutchinson and her followers settled Portsmouth in 1638; and in 1639 a splinter group from Portsmouth arrived in Newport.

Massasoit sold land to both Plymouth and Massachusetts Bay for their new towns. In each of his land dealings, however, Massasoit reserved from sale his headquarters at Mount Hope. Land-greedy Plymouth settlers authorized their agents to purchase all the Indian land that they could. But the Mount Hope Neck, the traditional core of Wampanoag lands and the tribal seat, remained unavailable. When Massasoit died in 1662, large areas of what had been Wampanoag lands surrounding the Mount Hope Neck were occupied by white settlers. Now, Massasoit's successor chiefs felt keenly the pressure of the encroaching white settlements.

KING PHILIP

The noble bearing of Metacomet (King Philip), sachem of the Wampanoag.

Chapter One

Montaup and Metacomet

The first permanent relationship between the Native Americans of New England and the white strangers was on a basis of peace and amiability. Massasoit, great sachem of the Wampanoag, personally welcomed the ocean-weary Englishmen as they set foot on the shores of Cape Cod Bay. For more than forty years, Massasoit remained a staunch friend of the white man. It must be remembered that when Roger Williams was forced to flee from his Salem home into the frozen wilderness, it was Massasoit who gave him shelter and hospitality. At that time, Massasoit was making his headquarters at Sowams (Warren) or at Pokanoket (Montaup/Mount Hope).

In 1639, three years after the founding of Providence, Massasoit brought his eldest son Mooanam, otherwise called Wamsutta, to Plymouth, and solemnly renewed his pledge of peace and friendship with the colonists. This stalwart native prince and his young brother, Metacomet (Philip), thereafter grew to manhood in an era of peace while the whites continued to force the natives farther and farther back into their hunting grounds. Both Wamsutta and Metacomet shared their father's trust in the strangers, and even though certain treaties and compacts were not always observed to the letter by the colonists, upon the death of Massasoit, in 1661 or thereabouts, his sons continued to profess goodwill toward the English. Wamsutta, the successor to the position of sachem, presented himself before the Plymouth authorities and by his request received the name of Alexander, while his younger brother requested and received the name Philip. Both assumed names that had been those of Macedonian kings and conquerors.

Shortly after he assumed control over the Wampanoag Nation, the domain of which extended from Narragansett Bay east to Plymouth and included much of present southern Rhode Island and Massachusetts, Alexander was suspected of engaging with the Narragansett in a plot to unite the scattered, disorganized Indian tribes in New England. Innocent of the charge or not, the youthful sachem was taken to Plymouth by force, where he was compelled to undergo harsh questioning and other indignities. According to records, this ordeal threw him into a fever (possibly poisoned by the English) from which he never recovered. Whatever may be the cause, Alexander died in the custody of his inquisitors, and this tragedy proved to be a turning point in destiny that led directly to untold death and destruction. The young brother Philip then became sachem, and upon the occasion of assuming the high office of ruler, there was a great gathering of chiefs and warriors at an extended feast of rejoicing at Philip's home and tribal headquarters, Mount Hope.

King Philip began his reign by renewing the treaty with the English made by his father and ratified by his brother. Then, for nearly a decade this proud, ambitious chief, angered at the circumstances of Alexander's death, ruefully watched the rapid spread of the whites, saw their infidelity and at last he complained to the English of trespasses upon the planting lands of his people. The matter was settled for the time being, but there was only one course left open for one who was unwilling that his country be completely taken over by those he was justified in regarding as—armed resistance. Secretly Philip's emissaries journeyed far and wide organizing a widely scattered people to the point of engaging in warfare. King Philip proved to be highly qualified for the undertaking; he gained the alliance of the Narragansett and quickly extended his league of rebellion far to the west among the tribes near the Connecticut River and beyond. For much of the time he remained at Mount Hope, making plans for actual battle, seeking advice from trusted allies, receiving and entertaining messengers from distant tribes and feeding and arming unattached warriors who volunteered to fight in his cause.

First Blood

Tradition says that the Indians believed the antagonist who drew first blood was doomed to defeat. So it was that some of Philip's men wandered openly in an aggressive manner, endeavoring to cause the English to fire upon them. They did not have long to wait; the English, on tenterhooks for Indian scalpings, had itchy trigger fingers.

It is written in Swansea, Massachusetts records that William Salisbury and his twenty-year-old son John are responsible for beginning the war. On June 23, 1675, William ordered his son to shoot one of three Indians seen running out of his empty house, which he had previously abandoned when he and his family fled to Rhode Island. Young Salisbury fired, his bullet striking one of the intruders. Some historians say the Indian was killed, others say he was wounded. Regardless, the result was the drawing of first blood and Philip had his reason to declare war upon the English.

For Philip, first blood was drawn and in his mind revenge and victory were his; thus, on June 24, 1675, the tragic conflict known as King Philip's War began in the village of Swansea near Mount Hope. Several men were killed by Philip's warriors, and all the dwellings in the village were destroyed. All New England was aroused and quickly sought to provide protection against further attacks. Thus began the longest, bloodiest and least chivalric war that the colonists had yet waged with the Indians, mostly at the hands of Massachusetts and Connecticut whites and their Christian Indian allies, the so-called "praying Indians."

A party of Plymouth foot soldiers and horsemen started in the direction of Mount Hope expecting to find Philip, but he had abandoned his camp. While the English lost valuable time making plans to build a fort on Mount Hope, the Indians were spreading

The death of King Philip.

death and destruction in all quarters. Throughout the summer every white person in New England was in constant danger of sudden death. Guerilla warfare prevailed most of the time, with the Indians firing upon the whites from the cover of underbrush. Often the natives would descend upon a small village or plantation, kill the inhabitants, young and old, plunder the dwellings and leave everything in ashes. Mendon was destroyed in July and Brookfield was viciously attacked in August. On the first of September, Haley and Deerfield were put to the torch, and shortly after, ten men were killed in Northfield. The last raid of consequence, upon Hatfield, occurred in October. With the approach of winter most of Philip's warriors and their families went into hiding on an island in the depths of the Great Swamp in South Kingstown, Rhode Island.

On December 19, 1675, occurred one of the bloodiest and most brutal massacres recorded in the history of New England. Practically all the occupants of the frozen swamp village were killed by an enraged, well-organized and well-armed force of colonials. The colonists' massacre, amounting to genocide, practically annihilated the

Native American population in these parts, thus ensuring the newcomers unchallenged dominion. It should be noted that the army raised in Plymouth for the singular purpose of this attack consisted of men from the colonies of Plymouth, Massachusetts Bay and Connecticut. Very few men from Roger Williams's Providence Plantation or Portsmouth took part in the action.

Several months later, Captain Benjamin Church from Little Compton (then part of Plymouth Colony), a military leader drafted by the Plymouth government, learned that Philip had returned to his favorite haunts after months as a fugitive in the wilderness.

The August 12, 1676 sneak attack and murder of King Philip at the cold spring on Mount Hope is an often-told story and it is generally well known, but its chilling details are better told by the authors noted in this book's bibliography. Like all wars with America's indigenous people, the tale of King Philip's War is filled with strange mixtures of barbarism and heroism, the Indian warrior often rising in the pursuit of his ideal to a moral grandeur that his "civilized" antagonist failed to attain.

On that fateful day, Church with a force of colonists and so-called "praying" Indians, defectors from Philip, hurried to Mount Hope and lost no time in cornering the proud chief at the foot of the summit. As the weary, hungry, disillusioned leader of a conquered race knelt to slake his thirst from the cool water bubbling from a spring, a shot rang out, and Metacomet, son of Massasoit, fell dead. Ironically, one of his own people fired the fatal bullet that closed the career of a true patriot, a man who was ready to fight and die for his country.

An Alternate Account of the Events of August 12, 1676, at Mount Hope

The often-chronicled story of the death of King Philip by the action of Captain Benjamin Church in the miry swamp at Mount Hope may not have been accurately recorded. Many members of the Pokanoket clan believe the tribe's traditional oral history traces the actions leading to the escape of King Philip and his son.

It is told that preceding Church's advance on Mount Hope, where Philip had taken refuge, Church met with an encampment of Pocasset Wampanoag to gain intelligence of Philip's whereabouts. At that time, in the presence of many Pocasset, Church swore an oath that he would not harm a "hair upon Philip's head."

Church reasoned it was in the interest of the colonists and of the Indians to end the long and bloody war. Church knew if word went out of the death of Philip, the warriors who followed him would disperse. So the plan was put into motion that a traitor, a Pokanoket named Sassamoan, was executed. His face was disfigured, and he was decapitated and his body quartered. For the subterfuge to succeed, Philip's warriors must believe the dead man was indeed their leader. As a means of identification, Philip's wampum belt was placed on the body.

In the meantime, colonists and Indians loyal to Church escorted Philip and his son to Connecticut, where word of Philip's death had preceded them. When challenged by a party of Mohegans, Philip raised his war club and challenged to battle five of

Captain Benjamin Church of Tiverton and Bristol is remembered as the vanquisher of King Philip.

the strongest braves. At this, the Mohegan recognized Philip and, thinking him to be a ghost, fled and left the travelers in peace.

Oral tradition continues that Philip and his son were given safe passage to the English West Indies colony of Bermuda.

It is also said that Philip's son was raised as an Englishman, and eventually came back to Mount Hope. The descendants of Philip's son are the Pokanoket people of today.

On a sunny August 3, 1924 afternoon, three young Bristol women display their pan filled to overflowing with quahogs dug from the stony beach at Bristol Narrows, a place also known as Pokanoket. During the early 1900s this was a popular summer retreat with modest, inexpensive cottages and a quiet way of life for working-class Bristol folks. No longer just for summer relaxation, the area is now choked cheek by jowl with permanent residences; a modest bungalow with a water view on King Philip Avenue was recently offered for $679,000.

Chapter Two

Settlement

In 1669, before the death of Metacomet, the general court of Plymouth Colony granted to John Gorham one hundred acres of land within the limits of the present town of Bristol on condition that it could be bought fairly from the Indians. This done, Gorham took possession of the land in 1671. After King Philip's War came to its tragic end, the grant was confirmed by the Plymouth Court and the land was given to Gorham and his heirs forever. The land was located on the peninsula or neck called Poppasquash. Thus, John Gorham became the first permanent white settler in what is now Bristol.

The colonials, hungry for arable land, now took steps to acquire Mount Hope and its surrounding environs for development. Three parties claimed the lawful ownership of the fertile Montaup lands. They were Massachusetts Bay, the Rhode Island colonies and an individual named John Crowne, and all three filed their claims with the sovereign.

John Crowne was a native of Nova Scotia, a poet and dramatist of some ability and a Royalist to the marrow. The French occupation of Nova Scotia had deprived his father of the property he held in that locality, and so John, who was somewhat of a favorite at court, requested the king to give the lands known as Montaup to his family as a consideration for their loyalty. His claim was considered with the others, and King Charles II granted the lands to the Plymouth Colony, conditional on a payment of seven bearskins per annum being made. Plymouth confirmed its ownership of the Mount Hope Lands. Bristol, with its well-protected harbor, was to play an important role in the economy of Plymouth Colony.

In January 1680 Plymouth sold the area "known by the name of Mount Hope Neck and Poppasquash Neck" to four wealthy Boston merchants—Nathaniel Byfield, Stephen Burton, Nathaniel Oliver and John Walley—who subsequently became known as the "Proprietors." Though the four proprietors were Bostonians, Bristol was still a town under the government of Plymouth Colony. Plymouth's civil government was managed by its freemen, or property owners, and by a representative assembly called the General Court. The Congregational church governed the religious life of Plymouth towns.

The proprietors immediately set out to develop the new town by inviting settlers. In August 1680, the proprietors and fourteen prospective settlers signed their Grand Articles, a kind of constitution of regulations by which they agreed to abide. The Grand Articles, in which the arrangement and requirements of the town and its buildings were set forth, was a rather unusual document for that period and time. Not only did it specify the plan of the town with its three principal streets—Thames, Hope and High Streets[1]—running parallel with the waterfront and of established widths, to be crossed by other streets at right angles that were also of specified widths and lengths, but it was further required that "all houses should be two stories high, with not less than two good rooms on a floor." The articles provided for 128 house lots. Further, the articles stated clearly that the town was being established "for purposes of trade and commerce!"

The center or compact part of Bristol was laid out as a grid, running east-west and north-south, a pattern that is still clearly visible. This pattern placed a green at the center for common grazing of livestock and drilling the militia. The Congregational church was located on or near the common so that the center of the settlement's spiritual life was also at its geographic center. Each eight-acre block formed by this geometric plan was divided into four house lots of about two acres each. The especially valuable lots along the waterfront were only one acre and were separated from the house lots by Thames Street. The clarity and geometry of the Bristol plan, a rarity in New England and a vivid contrast with the organic road patterns of earlier towns, is still a significant component of the town's importance.

The outlying areas of the town were divided into farms. In western, central and northeastern Bristol, most farms were about 100 acres; in the southeast, large 366-acre parcels were set aside for each of the four proprietors. Poppasquash Neck was laid out in long east-to-west strips to maximize the number of shoreline owners. Large areas of the town were left as undivided common land to be used for pasturage, for firewood and for sale to later settlers.

The first town meeting was held in September 1681, and seventy-six people were admitted to the town government as householders. As a precept in the Grand Articles, each householder received one or more house lots in the compact part of town, some acreage in the outlying area and a right to share in the common land. Captain Benjamin Church, the Indian fighter, was one of these new citizens. Recognizing the commercial importance of the town's harbor, the citizens renamed the Mount Hope Lands after the great English port city of Bristol.

In 1746–47, Bristol became a part of Rhode Island. Rhode Island had disputed ownership of Bristol against Plymouth and Massachusetts since the mid-seventeenth century. Terms of the settlement included present-day Cumberland, Tiverton, Little Compton, Warren and part of Barrington.

The Proprietors

Bristol is uniquely different than the other New England colonies. Its location in the Mount Hope Lands, with its harbor on Narragansett Bay, is nearly ideal. When the power of the native inhabitants was broken for all time at the close of King Philip's War in 1676, the founding of the new colonial town was inevitable. The town's founding was carefully undertaken as a sound business proposition. In the same year the Mount Hope Lands became the property of the Plymouth Colony by right of conquest, the colony sold that tract of land "commonly called Mount Hope Neck and Poppasquash Neck" to four prosperous Boston merchants, transferring ownership with the "turf and twig" ceremony that was then the common practice of real estate transferal.

The four proprietors had a chance to estimate the value of their purchase before buying. Thus they must have been reasonably sure of the success of their enterprise before paying the sum of £1,100 for the wilderness land.

There were four men of considerable means who signed the Grand Deed[2] of the Plymouth Colony and acquired the territory: John Walley, Stephen Burton, Nathaniel Oliver and Nathaniel Byfield. Many interesting things may be said about the Proprietors of Bristol. The most important of them was Colonel Nathaniel Byfield. He lived in the town for over forty years, during which time he exerted a major influence over local affairs, serving as chief justice in the Common Pleas division of the General Sessions Court for thirty-eight years. In that position he received five commissions from three English sovereigns—King William, Queen Anne and George II. He filled many other public positions in an efficient manner. Byfield held the office of first judge of the admiralty in 1705 and doubtless held the position many years, as he was in office in 1733 at the time of his death.

John Walley was a man of sterling character and pleasant disposition. He came to the New England colonies in 1660 at the age of sixteen and proceeded to establish himself as a respected citizen of Boston; he was frank in his estimates of the character of others, yet he had no personal enemies. After his part in planning the town, he was repeatedly a holder of town offices, but he never placed himself as a candidate for political office. He gained a reputation for performing all his duties faithfully. His opinions in matters pertaining to the good of the state of the plantation were often requested by political opponents. With the rapid rise in Bristol's economy, Walley increased his personal fortune; he was an ardent philanthropist and supporter of religious freedom. In later life he returned to Boston with greater wealth than that with which he left; he died there in 1712.

Stephen Burton was a scholarly man, the holder of an Oxford degree. Due to a temporary mental illness—probably depression—he played only a small part in the founding of the town. However, later he became very active in political matters concerning the town and the colony. It is said that because of his beautiful handwriting he was selected to serve as the first clerk of peace, a position similar to that of clerk of court. Additionally, he was sent five times to the General Court at Plymouth as a deputy representative from Bristol. He died in Bristol in 1693.

Nathaniel Oliver was one of the richest of the four, but he never settled in Bristol. He did, however, maintain a strong and tangible interest in the town even after almost immediately selling his interest as proprietor in the settlement to Nathan Hayman, a shrewd mariner-merchant of Boston. For his part in the development of the town as a commercial enterprise, Hayman can be credited with founding the maritime fortunes of the town. To this day, Hayman has never been admitted to the roll of names of the original proprietors; regardless of citizens' cognizance of the fact, he is listed in the records of the first town meeting as an original proprietor.

One of the early settlers who figured in many disputes was Judge John Saffin, who married Rebecca Lee, the daughter of the first resident minister. Once he accused Walley and Byfield of graft, but in a famous "retraction" said if their actions were "not uprighteous," then he had done them wrong and had better have spared this "poetical notions and satirical expressions"—an apology that must have been more cutting than the accusations.

A few of the other prominent freemen are the following: Nathaniel Bosworth, a cooper and fisherman who was given free "wharfage" in 1722; William Throop, commonly known as "Goodman" Throop, boasted of being the first man to enter the town on a cart drawn by oxen; and Richard Smith, the first town clerk.

Rebellious Indignation

One particular part of the history of Bristol that is so interesting is that relative to the war between the colonies and the mother country. In the events preceding the Revolution, Bristol gave no uncertain sentiment regarding the course it intended to pursue. The town sent out a crew of armed men, under the leadership of Captain Simeon Potter, in company with John Brown the merchant of Providence, to assist in the destruction of the British schooner the HMS *Gaspee*, and the town's financial contributions flowed freely to the relief of distressed citizens of Boston.

Though there were some Tories in the settlement, the majority of the inhabitants favored the cause of independence, as the following incident endorsing the famous Boston Tea Party attests. In order to manifest their approval of throwing the tea overboard into Boston Harbor, a committee consisting of Joseph Russell, Nathan Fales, Simeon Potter, William Bradford, Shearjashab Bourne, Benjamin Bosworth and Joshua Ingraham was appointed at a town meeting held February 16, 1774, to draw up resolutions, which, upon approval by the town, were sent to the Boston Committee of Correspondence and printed in the *Newport Mercury*.

The document was a bulky one, full of "righteous indignation," which made it plain to all who read that "the blood of our ancestors is boiling in our veins." At the same time, confidence was expressed in the sovereign, George III, and it was wisely suggested that if the "wicked" were taken away from the court, "an happy era would commence" and "wisdom, justice, and clemency of administration would conciliate the affection of the colonies." In June of the same year a subscription of £48, 4s., 4d. was taken up in the town for the relief of the destitute in Boston.

Surely it was these actions and others, now lost to unrecorded history, which the British remembered when on October 7, 1775, the HMS *Rose* and several other ships of His Majesty's Navy dropped anchor in Bristol Harbor and unceremoniously commenced a bombardment of the town that lasted for several hours.

The male colonials of Bristol drilled weekly on the town common.

Grand Medal of Honor

AWARDED TO THE

Davis Vertical Feed

SEWING MACHINE,

AT THE

Centennial Exhibition,

PHILADELPHIA, 1876.

FOR SALE BY

Marcus A. Franklin

BRISTOL, R. I.

Chapter Three

Point Pleasant Farm

The history of Poppasquash Neck is long and rich, dating to the origins of the town. The fertile, verdant fields had been cleared of stones by many generations of natives who cultivated the soil; the marshes, tidal pools and shoreline were rich in marine life; and ancient woodlands made this finger of land a coveted place. Until the mid-twentieth century, Poppasquash was largely residence to Bristol's aristocracy, its so-called "Great Folks." Generally, only wealthy WASPs owned large tracts and built their grand homes on the east slope looking down upon the larger compact town across the harbor.

At the founding of the settlement in 1680, Nathaniel Byfield, one of the four proprietors, purchased many of the numerous Poppasquash farms until he owned almost the entire peninsula. Byfield was the richest and most influential of Bristol's four Boston proprietors. In addition to his Poppasquash holdings, Byfield also had deeds to Hog Island and several tracts of land on Bristol Neck, on one of which he built a grand town house. But he built his first house on the land that was later to be called Point Pleasant Farm, and he took residence there as early as 1681. After putting down his roots, Byfield lived the balance of his life in Bristol, although he died in Boston on June 6, 1733.

At one time the Poppasquash Road to Point Pleasant Farm was an avenue lined with mazzard cherry trees. Byfield had the trees brought to Bristol from Asia in half hogsheads, each half barrel filled with soil and little trees deeply rooted therein. It was told that when the trees were mature and in blossom, the pink-canopied road was one of the most beautiful sights in Bristol.

Sometime after Byfield's death, his heirs sold the Poppasquash property to William Vassal, a Tory from a prominent Massachusetts family. During the Revolution, Vassal's Royalist sympathies were well known to the citizens of Bristol, and on more than one occasion he was the object of stoning by townsfolk. The tale is told that when the Honorable John Adams was paying Vassal a visit, the two men walked along the shore of Bristol Harbor beneath the trees and Vassal announced that he was thinking of cutting down the trees. Adams replied, "If you do, it will be well to keep just one." Vassal asked why, and Adams said, "To hang yourself on." In October 1779, when

The Byfield-Vassal-Herreshoff house at Point Pleasant.

the British troops departed Newport, Vassal and two other families loyal to the crown fled Bristol onboard the departing ships.

In 1780, although the fighting had moved elsewhere, some French troops were still stationed in Bristol. French solders were quartered in barracks erected on the abandoned Vassal farm, and they were granted land for a burial ground; the bones of many French are presumed to still lie there.

In 1781, the Tory estates in Bristol, including Isaac Royal's Mount Hope Farm and the Vassal property, were confiscated by the state and later sold. John Brown, the merchant of Providence, bought William Vassal's Poppasquash farm. He paid slightly more than £3,293 for the 221 acres and all the buildings except the French barracks.

It is thought the name of Point Pleasant Farm was given to the old Byfield-Vassal property by John Brown, because that was what it was called when his daughter Sarah and her husband Karl Friederich Herreshoff moved there as newlyweds.

Shortly after the twenty-four-year-old Herreshoff, who was born in Minden, Prussia, arrived in New York in 1787, he anglicized his name to Charles Frederick Herreshoff. In New York, he engaged himself in the importing business and eventually this interest brought him to Providence, where he met wealthy merchant John Brown. Brown engaged the young Herreshoff in his Brown and Ives boat building operation. It was through this employment that Herreshoff eventually met and fell in love with Brown's daughter, Sarah. After an eight-year courtship (this eight-year courtship corrects the mistaken eleven-year courtship that is mentioned in *Herreshoff Yachts*, The History Press,

2007), Herreshoff convinced Brown to give his daughter in marriage. As a wedding gift, Brown gave the couple the elegantly furnished Point Pleasant Farm homestead. There, before 1812, five children were born to the Herreshoffs.

In 1819, while he endeavored to develop John Brown's Adirondack landholdings in Old Forge, New York, Charles Frederick Herreshoff's life ended by his own hand.

Charles Frederick's widow remained at Point Pleasant Farm until her death in 1846. Evidently, Sarah was an unusual and very resourceful woman for the early nineteenth century; to her credit, she was an accomplished musician, and she was proficient in mathematics and astronomy. It was Sarah who taught her children a love of boating. The couple's daughters, Anna and Sarah, also lived at the farm until their deaths in the 1880s.

Of the second generation of Herreshoffs, only Charles Frederick Jr. married. All nine of his children were born at Point Pleasant in the same house that Nathaniel Byfield had built in 1680. Charles Jr. was an inspired tinkerer; having inherited some of the Brown fortune, he was able to indulge his delight in mechanics and sailing. It was his offspring, the third generation of Herreshoffs, who would revolutionize the art and craft of sail- and powerboat design. Charles and his second wife, Alice,[3] lived at the farm until his death in 1917.

Charles B. Rockwell, director of the Cranston Worsted Mills, was born in Cranston, Rhode Island, in 1889. He was raised at 610 Hope Street in Bristol and his earliest friends were the sons of Nathanael Greene Herreshoff (Captain Nat). In the 1920s, Rockwell and his wife Eleanor built a house they called Rockledge on the southwest corner of Hope and High Streets, only one block from Captain Nat's spacious Love Rocks home.

Three years before his death in 1938, at age eighty-seven, Captain Nat designed the auxiliary yawl the *Belisarius* for his friend and neighbor, Rockwell, who was to be the future owner of Point Pleasant Farm.

The Point Pleasant farmlands eventually whittled down in multiacre tracts until only fifty-five acres of the farm remained on the literal point of land south of where the original house had once stood. The Byfield-Vassal-Herreshoff house burned to the ground on January 9, 1925, presumably by the careless tossing of a cigarette into the grass.

In 1938, Charles B. Rockwell bought fifty acres of the farm from the Herreshoff family. It is believed that the Rockwells began living at Point Pleasant on the same day that the 1938 hurricane struck, in a house designed for them by Bristol architect Wallis Howe.

In 1959, Norman Herreshoff, a direct descendant of Charles Frederick Herreshoff and Sarah Brown, sold the northern portion of the farmlands to Dudley Williams. The proceeds were specifically earmarked for a fund established for the rebuilding of Bristol's Rogers Free Library, which had been destroyed by fire in 1956.

The current use of Point Pleasant is that of an inn and resort. With additions and alterations, it is basically the same Charles B. Rockwell two-and-a-half-story, Tudor Revival country house, named for Nathaniel Byfield's 1680s dwelling that stood to the south.

The Charles B. Rockwell estate that is now Point Pleasant Inn.

HORSFORD'S ACID PHOSPHATE

LIQUID

FOR

MENTAL EXHAUSTION, DYSPEPSIA, HEADACHE, NERVOUSNESS, URINARY DIFFICULTIES, DIMINISHED VITALITY, &c.

Manufactured according to the directions of

Prof. E. N. HORSFORD.

BY THE

RUMFORD CHEMICAL WORKS.

E. N. HORSFORD. PREST.

PROVIDENCE, R. I.

N. D. ARNOLD. TREAS.

FOR SALE BY

CHAS. A. JOHNSON,

DEALER IN

FINE GROCERIES,

Cor. Hope and Franklin Sts., Bristol, R. I.

CHAPTER FOUR

POPPASQUASH NECK, REDCREST AND THE BRISTOL YACHT CLUB

On December 21, 1723, Proprietor Nathaniel Byfield sold 642 acres of his Poppasquash property to Samuel Viall. On June 12, 1749, Samuel Viall left one-half of this land to his daughter, Susanne Richmond, one-third to his grandson, Samuel Church, and one-sixth to his granddaughter, Martha Church. Viall sold two small parcels of land and left the remainder to his son Thomas.

Samuel Church married Anna Davis of Newport in 1755, and they had eight children. His son, Thomas, inherited the family farm (the Church-Manchester House, circa 1770), originally part of Nathaniel Byfield's 660-acre farm. Thomas willed the property to his sons Stephen T., Samuel W. and Hezekiah Church in 1843.

William B. Spooner had purchased a forty-two-acre plot of the Church land for $6,000 on March 20, 1837, from Thomas Warner, guardian for George S. Warner of Illinois. It is unclear as to how Warner acquired this property (it is assumed he inherited it from one of Susanne Richmond's or Martha Church's descendants).

With his brothers, Stephen T. Church purchased the forty-two acres from William B. Spooner for $6,700 on July 11, 1842, which includes the current Bristol Yacht Club property within its boundaries.

In 1860, Stephen T. Church sold approximately six acres to Mary West, whose husband James H. West, of Saunders & West Boatbuilders, erected the mansion called Redcrest. The mansion was so named because of the exterior colors of red with green trim. In 1869, Redcrest was sold to Oliver Hazard Perry (grandson of Commodore Oliver Hazard Perry), whose widow Mary sold it to Theodora DeWolf Colt in 1879.

In 1880, New York Governor Kortright bought Redcrest and the adjacent land, and in 1886 turned ownership over to his mother, Sarah A. Taylor. Mrs. Taylor soon set out to enlarge and improve her new home. She added a hexagonal turret on the east side, a three-story tower with cresting on the west, a wraparound bracketed porch with elaborate three-story portico on the harbor side and a large ell on the north. Mrs. Taylor sold the property to the Wardwell family in 1921.

It was with a sense of anticipation that the executive committee of the Bristol Yacht Club signed an option with the Bristol Yacht Yard on a three-acre piece of land on Poppasquash Road containing the old rundown Redcrest mansion.

Redcrest, circa 1925. This house began as a simple summer residence in the mid-1860s; over its several decades of existence it was greatly enlarged and ornamented by its many subsequent owners.

The Bristol Yacht Club moved into its new quarters on the footprint of Redcrest, June 26, 1955. This photo is circa 1998.

The original sales agreement was for $15,000; however, numerous obstacles were encountered in trying to obtain clear title to the land. The August 6, 1954 *Bristol Phoenix* quotes yacht club Commodore Miller as saying, "The purchase of Redcrest is improbable due to the legal snags."

After Hurricane Carol swept through town on August 31, leaving in her wake a tangled mass of wreckage in Bristol Harbor, the Bristol Yacht Yard went out of business and its property went up for auction on November 22, 1954. The primary mortgage holders were Samuel C. and Edith B. Wardwell, who had established the yard in 1921. Mr. Wardwell bought the property at auction for $18,000. The only

other bidder was Charles J. Falugo. Wardwell said that the Bristol Yacht Club would develop the southern part of the property (upon which Redcrest was situated). The closing was on February 4, 1955.

The Bristol Yacht Club, organized in 1877, moved from its quarters at the foot of Constitution Street to its new clubhouse on Poppasquash Neck on the west side of Bristol Harbor in 1955. Of the yacht clubs with clubhouses still in existence on Narragansett Bay, the Bristol Yacht Club is exceeded in age only by the Rhode Island Yacht Club.

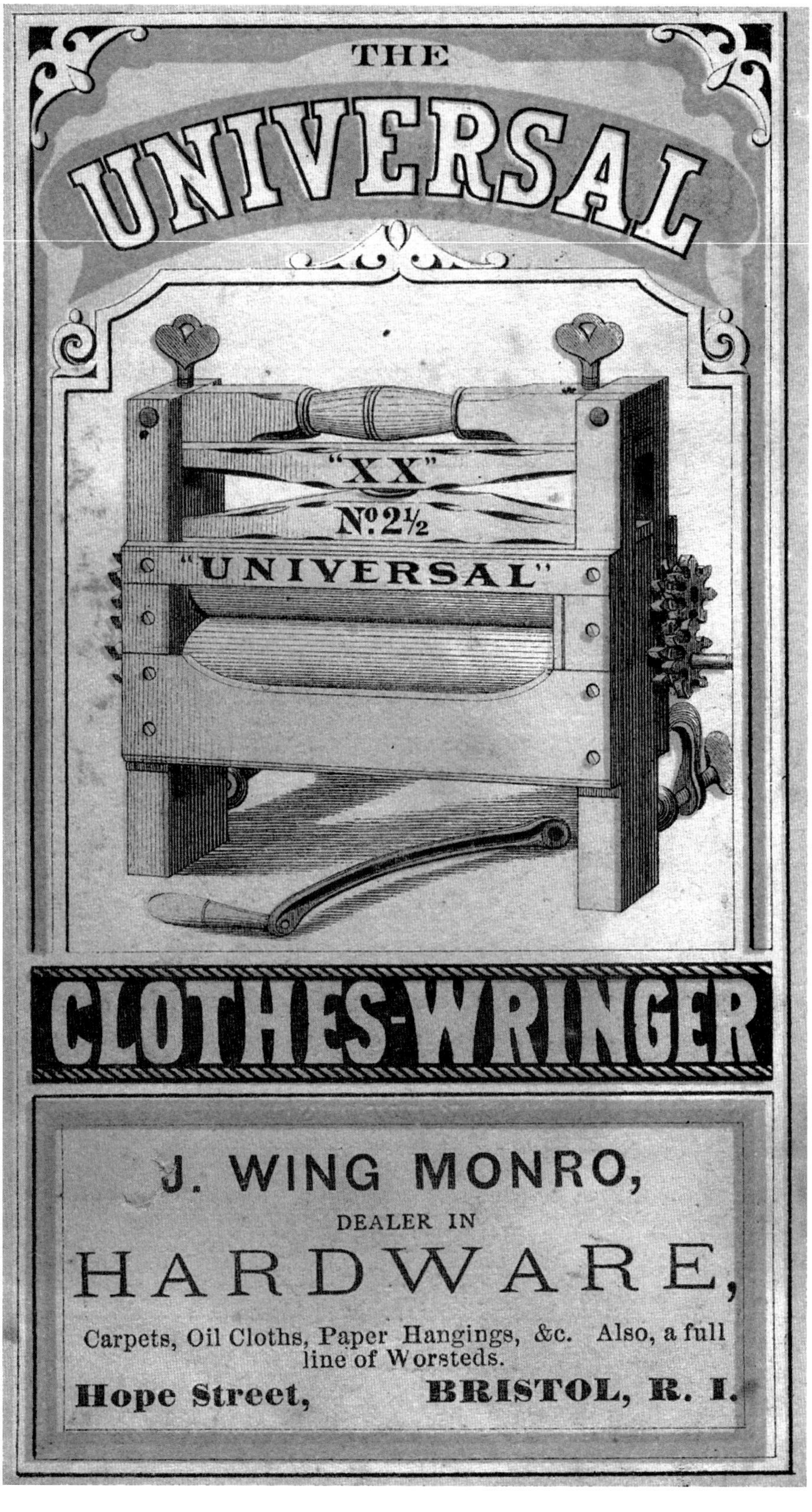
THE
UNIVERSAL
"XX"
No. 2½
"UNIVERSAL"
CLOTHES-WRINGER
J. WING MONRO,
DEALER IN
HARDWARE,
Carpets, Oil Cloths, Paper Hangings, &c. Also, a full line of Worsteds.
Hope Street, BRISTOL, R. I.

Chapter Five

Commerce

When the sea was Bristol's avenue of commerce, her harbor was the source of her livelihood. Like other New England communities, the town began at the water's edge and spread inland.

Bristol Harbor may be described as being formed by a long peninsula that juts southward at the northern end of Narragansett Bay and separates the two terminals of the bay, which project to the northwest and to the northeast like the forks of a gigantic Y. The northwest fork terminates in the Providence River; the northeast fork begins with Mount Hope Bay and leads to Fall River, Massachusetts, and the Taunton River. The peninsula known as Bristol Neck, separating the ends of the neck so that they look like the claws of a lobster, is Bristol Harbor. The harbor is partly protected by Hog Island at its entrance. It is not a snug anchorage in sou'westers and sou'easters. However, during the seventeen to nineteenth centuries, it was wide and deep enough to shelter many large merchant ships, coasting traders and fighting military and privateer sailing craft at the same time.

The historic waterfront site between Washington Street and Franklin Street was the location of Bristol's first commercial wharf, constructed for Parker Borden in 1722. Another town wharf was built by Nathaniel Bosworth in 1728 at the foot of Oliver Street. By 1851, four wharves had been built along this section of Thames Street: the Thompson Stanton Shipyard, the R.T. Butt Factory's Wharf, Church's Wharf and Peck's Wharf. When the Providence, Warren & Bristol Railroad opened in 1855, its station was built on Church's Wharf. In 1870 the site was enlarged by infill and a terminal for the New York Steamboat Wharf was built on a railroad spur. A crescent-shaped train shed, designed by Thomas Tefft, stood just south of the depot. Scheduled passenger service was discontinued after the 1938 hurricane. Freight service continued on an "as needed" basis into the early 1970s. The Town of Bristol now leases the depot site from the State of Rhode Island for its waterfront Independence Park.

It appears that the earliest stage of sea trade followed trade routes already established by larger ports; Bristol ships carried goods to and from ports along the East Coast and the Caribbean. The principal exports—horses, sheep, geese, onions and pickled

Premier THREAD COMPANY

fish—show that Bristol's skippers could draw on an agricultural surplus to produce their exports, and that some Bristol residents were engaged in commercial fishing.

Within only a few years of settlement, Bristol's farm crops and livestock were being shipped out of the harbor. One of the earliest recorded ventures occurred in 1686, when Nathaniel Byfield shipped horses and onions to the West Indies aboard his *Bristol Merchant*. This was Bristol's first sloop, and its commission by Byfield essentially established Bristol's first shipyard. At the early date of 1690, fifteen vessels were owned by town residents engaged in foreign commerce. A modest shipbuilding industry started in the 1690s; in 1696, the Bristol-built merchant ships *Grampus* and *Dolphin* were launched.

That number steadily increased until 1770, when fifty vessels were owned and manned at this port. At the start of the War for Independence, Bristol's seaborne trading enterprises were widely known and respected. By 1780, the town's commerce and prosperity were of considerable importance to the entire region. So important had Bristol become as a port of entry that a post office and customs house were established. In 1819, as many as one hundred ships were Bristol-owned. These consisted of West Indian freighters, seaweed sloops, slave traders and vessels carrying ice and onions to Cuba. Until the mid-1800s, Bristol Harbor was a nest of whalers, slavers, privateers and smugglers, or as the Bristol gentry referred to themselves, "free traders."

The principal trade of the vessels outfitted in Bristol—as well as Providence, Newport and Warren—was in rum, slaves and molasses. The best-established and most profitable voyages were made upon the simple plan of sailing the "first leg" of the voyage to Africa with hogsheads of rum and gaudy trinkets designed to appeal to primitive natives. Along the African coast, the slave ship skippers would anchor until they were able to exchange this cargo for natives. With holds filled with human cargo, they would set out upon the "middle passage" to the West Indies. In the several British and Spanish Caribbean colonies, the Africans were in turn exchanged for molasses, sugar and cash. The third stage of the voyage consisted of the run back to Bristol, where the molasses was distilled into rum and the ships would be reprovisioned and sailed off upon their triangular ventures again.

This was a very profitable trade, as evidenced by the many large established fortunes of the various New England seaports. At one time there were five distilleries in Bristol, while the value of its trade with Africa, the West Indies and the Spanish Main made its wharves busy with men and covered with warehouses from the early years of the settlement. By 1774, Bristol had a population of 1,209, of whom 114 were blacks. This number increased to some 1,600 by the end of the century and to fully 3,000 by 1820.

In 1804 the Bristol ship *Juno* arrived from Canton, laden with a cargo of teas, silks, porcelain, etc., valued at about $80,000. Duties were paid on this cargo amounting to $26,124.

Between the years 1801 and 1825, foreign ship arrivals averaged fifty annually, and in 1810 reached a record ninety-six. At the beginning of the War of 1812, Bristol was at the zenith of her commercial prosperity and wealth. Because of the war, trade diminished considerably. For some shipowners the war became another opportunity to gather wealth. With letters of "marque and reprisal" from the state, they began profitable operations as privateers, a form of legal piracy.

The expansion of Bristol's sea trade was dominated by the aggressive leadership of a few prominent families: the Bordens, the Bournes, the Wardwells and the DeWolfs. These families brought capital, experience and a wide variety of personal, commercial and political contacts to the maritime economy. Bristol shipowners, ship's captains and investors in the enterprise became very wealthy. Members of families organized partnerships, purchased goods, outfitted ships, planned complex voyages, took large risks and in many cases reaped great profits.

From 1825 to about 1850, the whaling industry was carried on to a considerable extent. After noting the success of whaling in other ports, certain investors turned their interests in that direction. As a result a ship was purchased and sent out, experimentally, to search for whales on the Pacific Coast. The venture turned out so well that a new industry sprang into being. At one time thirty-four vessels were engaged in this business in Bristol.

The maritime economy provided work for much of the town's population: clerks, teamsters, coopers, shipwrights, sailmakers and others. Many citizens made their living from the sea even if they never set sail. Bristol workers outfitted and serviced boats, helped to finance voyages, traded and repackaged cargoes, distilled the rum that was a principal export and worked at any of the town's four ropewalks. In short, while a few families and individuals led the maritime economy, many of the town's residents were dependent on and connected to the single economic base. The West Indian trade continued to flourish up to 1865, at which time it almost wholly ceased.

Industrious Bristol

Bristol has been engaged in various manufacturing industries during nearly the entire period of its history. The earliest manufactory of which we have knowledge, next to Wilkins's pottery, is the making of malt liquors by John Cary in 1681, in his Malt House Lane[4] brewery.

This was followed by other breweries and stills manufacturing malt liquors and rum. These businesses survived for about one and a half centuries before they wholly ceased. Several gristmills have operated in the town, some operated by tidal dams and some by wind power. The oldest mill of which there is a record was built by Joseph Reynolds, sometime prior to 1700, on Bristol Neck. After about twenty years it was moved farther south to the head of the harbor, at the place still called Windmill Point.

Shortly after the decline of the West Indies trade, new industries such as the manufacture of rubber goods, cotton cloth, rifles, sperm oil, refining of sugar and boatyards for cargo and pleasure craft were founded.

For a long period, swift sloops, shallow-draft coasters and large cargo shipbuilding occupied a prominent place among the industries of Bristol, employing large numbers of men and able-bodied boys. This industry had its greatest prosperity from 1830 to 1850. During a period of twenty-six years, some sixty commercial vessels were built and rigged. The business, which had declined in 1856 materially, increased when the

The 1903 Herreshoff-built America's Cup defender, the *Reliance*, was said to be the fastest sailing yacht in the world. *Period postcard.*

Herreshoff Manufacturing Company began building sailing and steam yachts and service vessels for the U.S. Navy.

The Herreshoffs, noted for their swift sailing craft, began commercial production in 1863. For about ten years, schooners and sloops were the company's sole product. In 1873, the character of the business changed from sailing to steam craft. All the vessels built by this boatyard are noted for their superior construction and speed. A well-deserved international reputation and sales developed, and production of fast, lightweight military vessels continued until the end of World War II. At the outbreak of the Spanish-American War in 1898, the Herreshoff boat works was building all-steel, seagoing torpedo boats for the U.S. Navy.[5]

The National India Rubber Works, located at its plant on Wood Street in 1840, was one of the largest concerns of its kind in the country. Its product included rubber goods of all kinds, but especially shoes and boots. During its peak production, twelve hundred hands were continually employed. In 1888, it was reorganized as the United States Rubber Company. The product line expanded to specialize in canvas rubber footwear. In 1918, production reached a daily output of fifty-three thousand pairs and employment reached three thousand.

The Namquit Steam Cotton Mill was erected in 1836, burnt in 1843 and rebuilt the same year.

A sugar refinery was established in 1849 by C.R. Diman & Company.

The Collins and Aikman Company was established in 1866 as the Cranston Worsted Mills by Charles B. Rockwell.

Herreshoff's magnificent J-class racing yachts always guaranteed a gathering of curious townsfolk at the waterfront on lower Hope Street. Here, the 1930 America's Cup defender, the *Enterprise*, is undergoing some overhaul.

The United States Navy's first all-steel, seagoing torpedo boat, the *Cushing*, which saw service in the Spanish-American War, was built by the Herreshoff Manufacturing Co. in 1886. *Period postcard.*

The main entrance to the National India Rubber Co. on Wood Street, circa 1880. *Period stereo view card image.*

This circa 1880 image is believed to be in the vicinity of the Cranston Worsted Mill between Constitution and Church Streets. *Courtesy of the* Bristol Phoenix.

John Wilkins, a Potter

For a variety of reasons, the potter's craft did not flourish in Rhode Island. One reason is the local clay is not of the best quality for sculpting. Most importantly, Rhode Island was amply supplied with earthenware from neighboring producers. The Berkley and Somerset potters, sailing in their sloops down Mount Hope Bay, captured a major part of the eastern Rhode Island market. The potters from Connecticut and Pennsylvania, trading along the Long Island Sound and into Narragansett Bay, garnered the balance of the business.

Notably, the first commercial potter in seventeenth-century Rhode Island was John Wilkins. He worked in Boston from 1670 to 1680 and then moved to Bristol as a pioneer settler of the town. Deeds found in town records leave no doubt that for a time, at least, Wilkins continued in his trade at the new settlement, but he met with no great success.

On March 4, 1685, he and his spouse mortgaged all their Bristol possessions to the four Boston proprietors. These lands included "all that their farme [*sic*] tract or parcel of Land containing 100 acres distant from said town [of Bristol] about a mile and a halph [*sic*]." Their lot consisted of twenty-four acres on Poppasquash Neck and one acre one and a half miles from Bristol center, all of which were then "in tenure and occupation" of Wilkins. The large farm tract stood between the country road to Swansea and the Swansea River and was bounded on the north by land of William Ingraham and south by William Brenton. This was the Wilkins homestead and presumably the location of his pottery.

On August 6, 1686, the town gave Wilkins permission "to keep an Ordinary, or Publick [*sic*] House of Entertainment." He is mentioned in this respect in 1689 in the diary of Samuel Sewall. As late as 1689, Wilkins was still called "potter." In the following year he sold his original holdings at Mount Hope to Israel Wardell and thereafter, in other transfers of land, he is referred to as "yeoman."

John Wilkins's daughter Abigail married Benjamin Ellery, one of Newport's most prominent merchants and ancestor of William Ellery, who signed the Declaration of Independence. The Ellerys lived in high style, with several black servants.

Wilkins died some time before 1711. His widow passed away at their daughter Abigail's home in Newport.

A view of the west end of the Old Academy. The image shows the location of the building on the town common just north of the Byfield School. The building was erected in 1791 for use as a private school. In 1830 the building was given to the town by James DeWolf and it was used as a public school until 1873. Later, the building was sold at auction, cut in two and the halves were moved to other locations in town. *Courtesy of the* Bristol Phoenix.

Chapter Six

A Summary of Public Education for Two Centuries

The history of education in Bristol properly begins with the old "grammar" school and also includes an academy and normal school. Tradition tells us that John Cary was the first schoolmaster. But according to reliable records compiled by Miss. Ellen R. Luther in 1876, Samuel Cobbitt was the first man engaged by the town to "instruct youths in knowledge." Cobbitt came in 1685; town authorities reserved a parcel of land for his use, and it was approved that his salary be twenty-four pounds per annum, each child having to pay three pence per week.

As seen in the following paragraphs, from town records, steps were taken at the fourth town meeting, held September 7, 1682, to provide for the education of children.

"Voted, that each person that hath children in town ready to go to school shall pay 3d., the week for each child's Schooling to a School master, and the Town by Rate according to each Rateable Estate shall make the wages amount to twenty-four pounds the year. The Select Men to look out a Grammar School master and use their endeavor to attain £5 of Cape Money granted for such an end."

Samuel Cobbitt was the master engaged to teach under this vote, and a house lot, a ten-acre lot and "commonage" were purchased for the schoolmaster. Cobbitt taught from 1685 until 1694; he was also employed by the town as a law enforcement officer (constable), rater of estates (tax assessor) and grand juryman. Cobbitt was succeeded by Josiah Hervey at an annual salary of twenty-five pounds.

At this point there is a lapse in school records and the next name recorded as schoolmaster is that of Mr. Easterbrooks in 1698. In that year the town was divided into two school districts, the Silver Creek being the dividing line; schools were established in both districts. In 1702, the sum of twenty pounds was appropriated to build a schoolhouse in the compact part of the town. Prior to that time, classes had been held in private residences. The plan was for Easterbrooks to teach on Bristol Neck (the North District) the three winter months and in town the remainder of the year. This plan did not meet with his approval and it was abandoned.

After a turnover of two or three teachers employed for short duration, Samuel Howland was chosen as schoolmaster in 1709. Easterbrooks was succeeded in 1712 by Timothy Fales.

Half of the Old Academy building, now used as a residence, retains most of its Federal period accoutrements; it is located on the north side of Franklin Street, just east of High Street, next to Batista's Bakery. March 2007.

The other half of the Old Academy building, also used as a residence, is located on Prospect Street. This half did not fare as well as the Franklin Street half; it has been severely altered from its original Federal style. March 2007.

This is the North District School, circa 1900. *Photo by K. Herreshoff DeWolf, courtesy Herreshoff Marine Museum.*

The Northeast District Primary School, later known as the Mason School, as seen on March 22, 2007.

In 1714, Nathaniel Byfield, "for and in consideration of a due regard which he had for the advancement of learning and good education," conveyed to John Nutting, who was then teaching the grammar school, certain land that has ever since been known as the "School Lands." These comprise "a lot lying between Church and Byfield Streets; a lot at the east end of the town; a lot between State and Bradford Streets, and a lot on the main road to Warren." From the income of this land the schools were long supported without taxation of the citizens.

Among the teachers in town during the first half of the eighteenth century were Amos Throope, 1724–26; John Wight, 1728–40; Mister Hovey, 1740–42; Shearjashob Bourn, 1742–47; and other successors for short periods.

In 1727 the town bought a schoolhouse on the neck that was erected by private funds, and in the same year fifty pounds were appropriated to build a schoolhouse in town. It stood on King Street (Church Street) between the courthouse and High Street. During nine years, beginning in 1772 and ending in 1781, there was no schoolmaster engaged in the town.

In 1802 Peter Church, William DeWolf and William Coggeshall, with others residing on the neck area, petitioned the town meeting for permission to build a schoolhouse on the ten-acre lot on the main road (Hope Street) to Warren; the privilege was granted, and a twenty-two- by twenty-foot brick building was erected, which was used until 1841, when a new one was built nearer to town. In *Sketches of Old Bristol*, author Charles O.F. Thompson relates his memories of the old brick schoolhouse on the neck. "The small, square old schoolhouse of brick, which once stood on the main Bristol Neck Road. The doorstep and a few bricks still remain by the roadside. The old schoolhouse was one of the chief landmarks of Bristol Neck. It did not enjoy this distinction on account of its beauty and size, but simply because it was the 'Brick Schoolhouse.'" The building was in existence when Thompson visited it in 1830 at age four. Without a specific date, we may assume the building was still standing in 1888 because Thompson writes, "[In] the winter of 1837–1838 when we returned to [visit] it. After fifty years the boys and girls return upon occasion, just as young [in spirit] as they were then, and take their places behind the old notched desks."

In 1803–04 a new schoolhouse was built in the Middle District. This schoolhouse was located at Hope Street and Gooding Avenue. It was later replaced by the Taft School (1841).

In preparation of this history of early education in Bristol, I asked fellow town historian and author Raymond Castro (*History of Defiance Hose Co., No. 1 Bristol, RI, 1905–2005*) for information on the subject. Castro said the Middle District School is the easiest to locate: it is the relocated Taft School building that was at one time headquarters of the Defiance Hose Co. No. 1. The building was erected at the cost of $500 on a small plot of land that was part of the Town Asylum Farm. Today, the building's original site is marked by the small opening in the whitewashed stone wall on the perimeter of the North Burial Ground. In 1913, when Colonel S.P. Colt built the access road to his farm through the grand marble gate, he had the school building moved across the street to its present location. Another South District School built in the compact section of town is the one known by a later generation of Bristolians as the "Old Brick School House." It was located at the southeast corner of State and High Streets.

The lot behind the low section in the whitewashed wall on the west side of Hope Street, north of the Colt Park gate, is the land from which the Taft School was moved. March 2007.

The relocated Taft School on the east side of Hope Street, opposite North Burial Ground. *Courtesy of the* Bristol Phoenix, *circa 1940.*

In this 1928 photo members of the Defiance Hose Co., No. 1 muster at their Taft School building headquarters. *Courtesy of Defiance Hose Co., No. 1.*

As seen in this March 2007 photo, the old Taft School building is rehabilitated and is used as a meeting place for civic and fraternal organizations.

The Brick School House on the town common was built in 1809 as a cooperative effort of the town and the St. Alban's Lodge of Masons.

The Brick School House on the town common was built in 1809 as a cooperative effort of the town and the St. Alban's Lodge of Masons. The Masons occupied the second floor, and school classes were conducted on the ground level. Mr. Gushee's classes in the Masons' brick building were called the Select School until 1838, when other classes more advanced took that name and the one taught by him was relegated to the name Grammar School. After nearly a century of use, the building was torn down in 1895 to make way for a new school on the town common. The now-vacant Walley School was built on the footprint of the Old Brick School House.

In 1811 a committee was appointed to divide the town into districts and to report upon the advisability of leasing the school lands for a long period. The report recommended doing so, and also recommended the division of the town into three districts: the North, the Middle and the South Districts. Nearly all of the lands were leased for a long term, excepting that in the town, which was sold.

Citizens residing in the North District built a schoolhouse at their own expense in 1815; this was the first one in the district. Another building in later years known as the North District School was built in 1844. The exact location of this building is unknown. However, proof of its existence is documented by the 1902 photograph by Miss K. Herreshoff DeWolf.

About the year 1826, a certain Mr. Storrs founded a private school called the Academy. The Academy schoolhouse, a wood-frame building in the Federal style, was built in 1791 on the western perimeter of the town common, opposite Court Street. The school was a marked success, and in 1828 the school committee asked Storrs to take over administration as principal of all town schools and include female scholars in his classes; he accepted and the brick schoolhouse was enlarged for the purpose. Mr. Storrs was succeeded by John Cross and Cross was succeeded by James E. Hidden. In 1836, Dennis S. Gushee became teacher in the grammar school in the first floor of the Academy schoolhouse. The accommodations there were insufficient, and in 1837 classes were moved to the brick schoolhouse.

The year 1848 was an ambitious one for school building, as plans were being considered for four new schools. The Northeast District Primary School, later known as the Mason School, was constructed for $300. It served well until the mid-1940s. The building survives at its original location on Metacom Avenue, slightly southwest from Sherman Avenue; it now serves as a residence.

In 1851 a school for black children was opened, and in 1853 a second grammar school was established. Evening schools were first opened in the fall of 1871, one each for boys and girls. In that year steps were taken that eventually resulted in the erection of the Byfield School on the town common; it is a three-story brick building that cost the staggering sum of $40,000. This school building was first occupied in August 1873. By that date the high school, three grammar schools, three intermediate schools and the advanced primary school were in operation.

After the Byfield School was built, it was determined that the Academy building had outlived its usefulness. The building was sold at auction, the new owner divided the building and the halves were converted into dwellings. The two halves are in use today, one at 79 Franklin Street and the other at 14 Prospect Street.

The no-nonsense Bristol School Committee of 1910 consisted of (front row, left to right): Earle Mason, Mr. Young, Dr. W. Fred Williams, George Arnold, Superintendent John Post Reynolds, William Manchester and Chandler Coggeshall; (back row, left to right): Dr. Alfred M. Merriman, Dr. Howard W. Church, Dr. Russell Church, Orrin Wilson, Philip Brady, Colonel Merton S. Cheeseman and two unknowns. *Courtesy of the* Bristol Phoenix.

The Burton School on the lower east side of High Street; photo dated May 16, 1913. The penciled note reads, "Burton School House about 70 years old [circa 1843], where Mrs. H.W. Maxfield first went to school."

The Burton School's second-grade class in 1905. Roswell S. Bosworth, eventual owner and publisher of the *Bristol Phoenix*, is the boy on the right end, front row. Other children, in uncertain order are: William Gladdy, Russell Kenney, Alice Geisler, Tony Ferrara, Peggy Best, Sam Sherman and Lloyd Haines. *Courtesy of the* Bristol Phoenix.

After outliving its principal mission, the old stone Burton School building became a meeting place for the United Rubber Workers and other civic groups. Today, privately owned and modernized, it is a first-class residence. March 2007.

Teacher Hiring and Pay Plan—1938

In a move that is today frowned upon as gender bias, seven married female teachers were dropped from the permanent list of instructors in Bristol public schools by the Bristol School Committee at its June 13, 1938 meeting.

At the same meeting, four new appointments were made; the appointments were Miss Emily Xavier on a half-time basis as a teacher in home economics in the ninth and tenth grades, and Miss Eleanor B. Rae, Anthony E. Agatiello and Miss Jean Tobin as teachers in the elementary grades. Superintendent of Schools Elmer S. Mapes said following the session, which was held behind closed doors, "There is a possibility that some of the married women teachers might be re-appointed in the fall, if the enrollment at that time warrants it." The school board voted to cut the salaries of male teachers in the elementary school from $1,200 to $1,000 minimum, $1,700 to $1,500 maximum, and from $1,800 to $1,600 supermaximum. This was considered an economic measure, and was also done to bring the males' rate of salaries nearer to that received by female instructors.

The 1919 graduates of Reynolds School were segregated by sex. The girls taught by Miss Hill were Lena Abemante, Blanche Belmore, Frances Campagna, Dora Ruggiero, Emma Thiele, Elizabeth Marz, Emma Gaulet, Catherine Pierce, Carroll James, Catherine Downey, Nancy Sodini, Doris Bullock, Esther Kamison, Margaret McCallum, Eileen Moore, Jeannette Thomas, Irene Servant, Mary Archerio, Genevieve Lucy and Marion Jones. The boys taught by Mr. Bailey were Archie Galdue, George Sparks, Daniel Chase, Sydney Dunbar, Herman Vermette, Loin Kenney, Herbert Newman, Joseph Williams, Dana Eisenberg, George Trainor, Charles Farro, Carmine Maisano, Hugh Holmes, James Goff, Oscar Desrosier, Joseph D'Alesio, Henry Brown, Louis Mastri, James Ruggiero, Carmine Bruno, Nat Sparks and Ernest Castellino.

Linden Place. This view is through the east entrance to the house's west front entrance.

CHAPTER SEVEN

FEDERAL-ERA ARCHITECT RUSSELL WARREN

Famed self-educated Rhode Island architect and Bristol resident Russell Warren possessed the impeccable taste and intuitive psychology that made it his cardinal principle to express his ideas with clean refinement of line. Warren, who began his work in Bristol, largely for the DeWolf family, gave the town chaste and honest architecture, thereby imparting the indefinable charm of its home atmosphere, as well as most of its historic value.

Many gallons of ink have been expended in numerous publications on the grandest example of Warren's genius, the DeWolf-Colt mansion, Linden Place. Therefore, there is little need to write more here on the subject except to say the mansion was saved from various questionable commercial schemes and is now publicly owned and open as a historic and cultural center.

Two notable examples of Warren's genius must be mentioned. One is the DeWolf-Middleton–owned Hey-Bonnie Hall.[6] The house presented, until its end, a rare and delightful picture of the Northern house with Southern plan, reproducing in its new location the characteristic and generous "wings" of the old Virginia plantation house. Unfortunately, the hurricane of 1944 sent the front portico roof over the house and did other serious damage. The house was pulled down shortly after that.

The other is the Howe-Churchill-Diman House, affectionately known as Four Eagles.[7] This house, which remains well preserved in the center of the town, on the western side of Hope Street, intrigues passersby. It is another fine example of Russell Warren's work; it was built in 1807, and one of its owners was that singular Captain Benjamin Churchill, who commanded the privateer *Yankee*. While the exterior of this house remains unspoiled, and is one of the most familiar and well-known designs in town, the interior—also little changed—is among the simplest and perhaps least "architectural" products from Warren's pencil.

In his 1942 book, *Sketches of Old Bristol*, Charles O.F. Thompson relates in great detail (much more than quoted here) information about the Honorable James DeWolf's home, called the Mount:

Hey Bonnie Hall, the DeWolf-Middleton estate on Poppasquash.

The Howe-Churchill-Diman House, affectionately known as Four Eagles.

The mansion house [in back of Fox Hill, on the east side of DeWolf Avenue] *was built in the year 1808 and survived for almost one hundred years, until it was destroyed by fire on the 22nd of December, 1904.*

Built before the days of his great riches, his house was not looked upon as extravagant for a wealthy man, but remarkable for the beauty of its proportions and design rather than elaborate ornamentation. Most carefully finished in all its parts, for it was built in the days of hand work, it could stand inspection.

It was a large, three storied, rectangular structure, always painted white, with five great chimneys and a beautiful portico over the front door on the west side, with stone steps and wrought iron railings. To the east was a large wing with a great kitchen, never the least important part in those fine old houses. A door to the south formed the garden entrance and the east entrance opening from the hall, to a tiled and covered piazza, was most often used by the family for one of the entrance drives wound up to it under a great horse-chestnut tree. The lofty hall ran entirely through the house from east to west and in fine weather the big doors were thrown wide open early in the day and hospitably left so. A spiral mahogany staircase ascended from the first floor to a glass cupola on the roof, from which most of the state and a part of Massachusetts could be seen. Fine doors of Santo Domingo mahogany opened from the hall to the adjoining rooms and much of the woodwork was of the same beautiful wood. The drawing rooms occupied the entire north side of the house, with beautifully carved fireplaces of Carara marble. The walls were adorned by a Neapolitan artist, who spent much time there, with scenes from Paul and Virginia, a view of Laplance, and one with an avenue of royal palms from the senator's plantation in Cuba.

The southwest room was the "Green Room," so called, from the prevailing color, most beautifully furnished with rare French and English furniture. A delicately carved marble fireplace gave tone to the entire apartment. This was the most occupied by the family and often served as a music room. In the days of the senator, five great wood fires were always kept going in the cold weather besides the fires in the kitchen. It took one man's entire time to attend them and no wonder acres of woodland were required to keep them all going.

Structures in Bristol Known to Be Built by Russell Warren

86 State Street (1807), Briggs-Warren-Bache House
500 Hope Street (1810), George DeWolf House (Linden Place)
82 State Street (1810), E. Gifford-Nelson House
515 Hope Street (1815), W. Fales-Wardwell House; demolished 1961
92 State Street (1810), Warren–J. Adams-Bosworth House
601 Hope Street (1833), A. Fletcher-Horingh House; demolished circa 1950
641 Hope Street (1837), J.R. Talbot House
617 Hope Street (1838), Gardner-Dimond House
15 John Street (1840), J.R. Bullock-Barnes House; moved from Hope Street circa 1900
89 State Street (1848), J.R. Bullock–S. Allen-Wyatt House

Structures in Bristol Attributed to Russell Warren

355 Hope Street (1807), Governor Dimond-House (Four Eagles)
132 High Street (1811), O. Davol House
139 High Street (circa 1811), W.R. DeWolf House
240 High Street (1817), Old State House–County Court House
1200 Hope Street (1848), Dana Gibson House (Longfield)

The Briggs-Warren-Bache House, 86 State Street (1807). Russell Warren is known to have had special affection for this house; he dwelled in it for a considerable time.

THE BRISTOL STATEHOUSE FOUNDATION

proudly presents

Anthony Quinn

in

FALL RIVER OUTRAGE

A COURTROOM RE-TRIAL

STATE OF R.I. v. REVEREND EPHRAIM K. AVERY

~ 1833 ~

SUNDAY, NOVEMBER, 22, 1998

3:00 P.M.

Chapter Eight

Mr. Anthony Quinn's Bristol Performance

The reenactment of the *State of Rhode Island vs. Reverend Ephraim K. Avery* took place on Sunday, November 22, 1998, in the restored Bristol, Rhode Island County Courthouse.

Principal players in the cast of characters were distinguished actor, three-time Academy Award winner and Bristol resident Mr. Anthony Quinn in the role of Chief Justice Samuel Eddy; John C. Corrigan, Esq., as Chief Defense Counsel Jeremiah Mason; Sanford H. Gorodetsky, Esq., as Attorney General William Greene; William P. Dennis, Esq., as clerk of the court; Marilyn May as the ghost of Sarah Cornell; Jack Duff as Reverend Avery; George L. Sisson as Associate Justice Charles Brayton; and Paul Fletcher as Associate Justice Job Durfee.

On a brisk Sunday afternoon in November 1998, making his first public Bristol appearance since moving to town in 1995, internationally respected actor Anthony Quinn took his place at the judge's bench as Supreme Court Chief Justice Samuel Eddy.

Dressed in a judge's dignified black robe and brilliant white ruffled linen collar, with his leonine silver hair and close-cropped beard, Quinn looked every inch a nineteenth-century jurist. When he made his entrance the audience stood and applauded. As he moved through the crowd to his seat, the applause began to abate. Without turning his head, Quinn said, "No, no, keep it going, keep it going." And the show was on. The audience dispensed its approval with waves of applause and laughter until the star took his seat at the bench.

It was Quinn's courtroom, and to the delight of the audience, he did whatever he wanted. The trial itself featured a mixture of courtroom drama, sex, religion and scandal. In the end the defense won, and the jury, played by members of the Bristol Rotary Club, found the Reverend Avery not guilty.

However, before the jury's verdict was read, Quinn left his mark on the trial and on the memories of everyone in attendance. The actor rose and addressed the courtroom audience. "I am talking to you now not as the judge anymore, but as Bristol resident Anthony Quinn. I moved here to Bristol three years ago…and I have tried to fit in…I thank you all; you let me live like a normal human being here."

Members of the Bristol Rotary Club acted as members of the jury. The standing man is respected citizen the late Mr. George Yanyar; seated to his left is Bristol Town Clerk Louis P. Cirillo.

We Bristolians are not blasé, nor are we star-struck. We are respectful of our fellow citizen's privacy and enterprise. We also remember that our streets and lanes have been tread by the mighty and powerful—presidents, princes and privateers—during our three hundred years. So it is when Hollywood comes to Bristol we are apt not to gawk or intrude.

The eighty-six-year-old Oscar-winning actor, who made Bristol his home for six years, died in a Boston hospital on June 3, 2001. He is buried beneath his favorite maple tree on his Poppasquash estate.

Standing beneath a portrait of Proprietor Nathaniel Byfield, Mr. Anthony Quinn introduces his young son to the approving Bristol audience. Mr. George L. Sisson is seated to Mr. Quinn's right and to his left is Professor Paul Fletcher; in the foreground is William P. Dennis, Esq.

T. T. ALLAN,
Dry and Fancy Goods,
80 & 84 Hope St.,
BRISTOL, R. I.
270
COPYRIGHT 1881 BY F. TODD

Chapter Nine

Rights-of-Way to the Water[8]

The King Charles charter to the Rhode Island Colony of 1666 was the first document establishing a civil state based on religious tolerance. The charter also explicitly grants ownership of the colony's coastal waters to the people.

The principle of public ownership of coastal waters is carried through to Article 1, Section 17 of the Rhode Island Constitution, formulated in 1842. This explains why there is such emotion about maintaining a free and open access policy toward our marine resources.

In early September 1969, I requested and received from town engineer Joseph G.R. Riccio a list of twenty-five rights-of-way to the shore. I then made a tour of all the streets and lanes on his list, making notes as to the accessibility of each right-of-way. Next, my findings were sent to the town council and State Representative Michael J. Balzano, and to the editor of the *Bristol Phoenix*. In the same September 12, 1969 issue of the *Phoenix* in which my letter appeared, an editorial titled "Right-of-Way Crusade" indicted my findings as "waving the flag in behalf of social reform" for suggesting that "Bristol's rights-of-way are subject to abuse by special interests." Poppasquash Road was particular in this regard.

My letter to the editor kicked off a debate lasting nearly four decades. Some rights-of-way that were closed are now open, and through research of town records others were discovered.

A letter to the *Phoenix* by former Highway Surveyor Louis A. Castriotta Jr. added several rights-of-way to the twenty-five that I had listed. Castriotta also made some political commentary.

> *Some weeks back, an issue was raised in your columns by Dick Simpson i.e. the unknown or unmarked rights of way through out the town. The Town Council, paying lip service to the matter, instructed the Town Engineer to investigate the matter and report back. It should be noted that under the recent Republican regimes, the Town Engineer's staff has increased at least six fold. His report back to the council can be considered nothing more than an insult to those of us who pay wages for a*

> *professional engineer. The report was lacking in both accuracy and quantity maybe intentionally because of the parties involved.*
>
> *However, for the edification for the citizens of Bristol, I present herewith close to 50 rights of way. Starting from northwest corner of town and proceeding around to the northeast sector they are: Beach Road; Northwest of Peck Avenue; Aaron Avenue; Gibson Road; Fales Road; Town Beach; Asylum Road; Plat 168 between lots 8 and 9; Plat 168 between lots 9 and 10; Plat 168 to north bounding of lot 12; Poppasquash Road; Perry Street; Oliver Street; Franklin Street; State Street; Town Dock; Rockwell Park; Church Street; State Armory; Constitution Street; and Union Street.*
>
> *Also shoreline north of Burton Street; Walley Street; Tanyard Outfall; Low Lane; Ferry Road; Tower Road; Babbit Street; Clipper Way; Mount Hope; Annawamscutt Drive; Sowams Road (east); Plat 151 between lots 22 and 23; Southeast of Platt Street; Narrows Road; Harrison Street; Kickemuit Avenue; Smith Avenue; Sherman Avenue; San Miguel Drive; Fatima Drive; Franca Drive; Butterworth Avenue; North Street; Robin Drive to Leahy Pond and Hampden Road to Leahy Pond.*
>
> *I believe that a study of the following three would be fruitful: (1) Plat 74 between lots 16 and 19; (2) Plat 9 northern part of lot 24; (3) Plat 11 between lots 14 and 15.*
>
> *The Town Council need not pay thousands of dollars a year in wages for this information. It is all available in the Town Hall. Now they stand challenged to open these ways.*

Next, a letter to the *Phoenix* by Salvatore Rossi again brought up the Poppasquash Road question and also revealed an attempt by residents along Poppasquash Road to close the Surprise Hill Road entrance to Colt Park. The editor's note at the end of Rossi's letter is of particular interest.

> *A few residents of Poppasquash have shown their hand! The injunction against the state to not use the south entrance* [Surprise Hill Road] *to Colt State Park is a thinly-veiled attempt to close off the rest of the public highway, which is closed to the rightful owners, the public, piecemeal over a period of years.*
>
> *I do not profess to be well versed on all the legal aspects, but I do know one thing which perhaps has escaped the attention of these people* [who live on Poppasquash Road]. *That is that private interests do not acquire any more rights to a public highway by the fact that they claim to maintain it, than the public in general. In short, they never have the right to deprive the public from the use and enjoyment of these streets unless they are formally declared abandoned by act of the town fathers, and that has not been the case I assure you.*
>
> *Even the British would attest to the fact that Poppasquash Point is of great historical value by the fact that a fort was built there by the Colonials to fire on the British gunboats as they sailed into Bristol Harbor. So you see, it is one of the oldest streets in Bristol. It behooves the townspeople to take more interest in their beautiful town, because the day will shortly arrive when you will only be allowed to use the streets, which are of no particular interest to some unscrupulous individual*[s] *who come here with the interest of setting themselves up in a dynasty.*

> Phoenix *Editor's note:*
> *The road in Colt Park which is in controversy was never a part of the town or state road system. It was originally a farm road, and was improved by Samuel P. Colt when he developed Colt Farm. It came into public ownership a few years ago when the state purchased the farm. The forts (there were two forts) referred to* [in Rossi's letter] *were supplied by barge from the fort near Surprise Hill downhill to the shoreline.*

In the same October 3, 1969 issue of the *Phoenix* appeared a news item that declared the Surprise Hill Road temporarily closed. Judge Florence Murray of the Superior Court came to Bristol and viewed the access road in connection with a temporary injunction against the state. Several Poppasquash Road residents brought the suit claiming the state had reneged on an agreement to control park traffic. One of these complainants, Clinton J. Pearson, informed the court that he had given the state valuable options to property on Mill Gut in the deal.

The state built a new road system at the park, and closed off the access road leading to Surprise Hill when the new system was opened. Closure of the road was protested by Bristolians who preferred this entrance, and Director of Natural Resources John L Rego promised shortly thereafter that it would be reopened. The injunction asked that the road remain closed.

In the March 31, 1970 issue of the *Providence Evening Bulletin* there appeared a story by C. Elliott Stocker with the title "Shoreline Public Way Need Cited." In the article he reported on some 148 newly identified public rights-of-way to the tidal waters in twelve shoreline communities, including Bristol. The findings were from recommendations made to Governor Licht and the General Assembly in a massive report compiled by the Statewide Comprehensive Transportation and Land Use Planning Program for the Commission of the Discovery and Utilization of Public Rights-of-Way.

The commission, headed by Representative Anthony Giangiacomo of Providence, found there is no existing legislation dealing with shoreline property rights, except as to harbor lines. Court cases have left private ownership rights "not clearly distinguishable," and the report recommended "some type of uniform legislation" by the General Assembly to protect the public's rights.

Over a period of nine months, the Statewide Planning Program staff conducted detailed surveys of 148 public rights-of-way to the water. The character and usability of the discovered rights-of-way "vary considerably," the report acknowledges. "Some are no more than foot-paths to the water while others provide vehicular access to attractive fishing or boating sites," it says.

The four-hundred-page report that includes plat maps and aerial photographs cites "an apparent conflict in regard to ownership of shoreline property on the east and west side of the bay" and devotes six pages to court decisions. The dispute appears to have been resolved in favor of state ownership between high-

and low-water marks, it says. But it recommends that "a unifying statute should be formulated setting this discrepancy."

The commission holds the opinion that the ocean shore area to which the public has rights of use should extend not just between high and low tide but "between the low tide and the line of vegetation."

The report lists eighteen rights-of-way in Bristol with existing conditions and the commission's recommendations. The eighteen are: Beach (S-1), Gibson (S-2) and Fales (S-3) Roads; Constitution (S-4), Union (S-5), Wally (S-6) and North (S-7) Streets; Butterworth Avenue (S-8); Azalea (S-9), Fatima (S-10) and San Miguel (S-11) Drives; Shermon (S-12), Smith (S-13) and Kickiemuit (S-14) Avenues; Narrows Road (S-15); Sunrise (S-16) and Annawamscott (S-17) Drives; and Low Lane (S-18).

Bristol Rights-of-Way Spark Debate

On the evening of April 23, 1980, a two-hour meeting before the five-man Coastal Resources Management Council (CRMC) Subcommittee on Rights-of-Way was witnessed by many concerned citizens. Two rights-of-way in particular sparked debate. The first right-of-way drawing audience response was Gibson Road in the north end of town, where a fence erected by members of the Bristol Highlands Association prevented access to a grassy strip of land leading to the water.

According to the CRMC, the document examination indicates that "the Town of Bristol would appear to be the record owner" of the 50- by 135-foot strip of land above the high-water mark.

The president of the Bristol Highlands Association, Neil O'Brien, said there is an opening in the split rail fencing for those wishing to get to the water, and that "the opening has always been open."

The second right-of-way at issue that night concerned a lane or path extending west from the end of Low Lane. A frequent user of the path, Dorothy Enos of Cottage Street, claimed this was a public right-of-way, and that a sign so designating it had been removed. She requested that the town see to it that the pathway be maintained leading to the quiet, peaceful strand of shoreline that she enjoys.

John Miranda of Wood Street spoke out at the hearing and recalled how he used to drive his vehicle nearly down to the shoreline on Low Lane. "Now a dump truck has dumped rubbish down there," and he added that a tree had been felled "on purpose" across the road.

Greg Bennik, an attorney for abutting property owners, presented photographs to the subcommittee showing the path in question to be undeveloped and not maintained. He added that the footpath is used primarily in the summer months for residents who wish to gain access to the beach or go over to Hog Island. Bennik continued by summarizing a statement to the council of what the council had found in its title examination, that it could "find no deed to the town of any portion of Low Lane" or evidence of "any town action accepting the highway."

One abutter, Paul C. Nicholson of Low Lane, asserted that the undeveloped section of Low Lane that the CRMC might designate a public right-of-way was a private road and could be used only by the neighborhood's residents.

Salvatore Rossi and Joseph Proto both disputed Nicholson's claim. "It's one of those places where the neighbors have been trying to block people from getting to the water," Rossi said.

Proto said, "I never had any trouble using the right-of-way until the last few years, and that was from the neighbors down there. They blocked it up."

Frank Fulton of Monkey Wrench Lane, which is off Low Lane, said, "The flow of people down there indicates that it has not been used by the public."

It was mentioned at the hearing that the secluded road had been a longtime favorite spot for romantic encounters. This comment drew laughter from the audience. "I don't think anyone has ever been stopped from going down there," said Public Works Director Joseph Cavallaro.

Eventually, the CRMC designated a strip of land 25 feet by about 265 feet, from the end of Low Lane to Bristol Harbor, as public right-of-way S-18.

A front-page article in the September 25, 1986 issue of the *Bristol Phoenix* warned of an upcoming public hearing to discuss ten Bristol rights-of-way to the water. The next most controversial right-of-way claim concerned the Paul Sanroma property on Poppasquash Road, an area favored by fishermen and quahoggers. The land in question was near Sanroma's home on Poppasquash Road, where he had posted signs all over the marsh stating that it was private property.

Paul and Edna Sanroma purchased their house on Poppasquash Road, set on a fifty-thousand-square-foot lot opposite an entrance to Colt State Park, in 1971. The contested portion was the so-called "beach lot," a crescent-shaped strip of beach that curves between Poppasquash Road and Bristol Harbor like a miniature peninsula.

According to Poppasquash Road resident George Sisson, a CRMC member who had a great interest in public access to the shoreline, "in Rhode Island, the shoreline, up to the high water mark, is public." The rights-of way provide a way for the public to get down to the shore. He said there had been many complaints from people being kicked off the beach behind Sanroma's house. As far as the marsh area is concerned, "the land where he has these signs does not belong to him." Sisson added that once land is taken over by encroaching seas, it belongs to the state—the people.

While addressing the ten possible Bristol rights-of-way, including the Sanroma claim, Alan Goldman, attorney for CRMC, said, "My title search indicates in every instance that they are [public] rights-of-way." In the case of the Sanroma property, he said, it is claimed there is a right-of-way to the inlet cut off from the harbor by Poppasquash Road. What the CRMC would consider is that "there seems to be a right-of-way to the inlet."

More than fifty Bristol residents packed the small CRMC chamber in Providence to hear or give testimony. The Sanroma contingent spoke of property descriptions and a 1974 court case; the opposing side recalled the days when townspeople used the beach to quahog or picnic.

A parade of witnesses testified to the longtime public use of the beach lot. Nicholas Castigliego told of his family's use of the area to launch their commercial fishing boat; Joseph Securo related how he had used the area to access the shore to fish when he was a boy; John Marine said from the time he was five years old, fifty-five years ago, he used to go quahogging down there. Salvatore Rossi said when he was a child, "On the weekend, there were so many people there picnicking, fishing, it was like Coney Island."

Charlotte Church, whose great-great-grandfather owned the property during the Revolutionary War, indicated that it was the position of her father, John Church, that the property was owned by the Town of Bristol, and that for long periods of time her forebears had allowed public usage of this property.

The Sanromas' attorney argued that the public use of the beach in the past had not been because a right-of-way exists but because the previous owner, John Church, had allowed people to use his property

The CRMC subcommittee agreed with residents, saying that the parcel had been consistently used by the public for more than twenty years, a condition that must be met before any land is designated a public right-of-way. The subcommittee report dated February 24, 1987, concludes: "Therefore, the Subcommittee recommends that this parcel be designated as a public right-of-way and that the signs be taken down by the parties who testified that they put them up. Signed: Joseph T. Turco."

Additional Bristol public rights-of-way to the water approved by the CRMC at their June 11, 1991 meeting included:

- Arron Avenue, a thirty-foot-wide L-shaped strip that stretches east from Narragansett Bay and then north. The parcel is bordered by the East Bay Bicycle Path.
- Peck Avenue, a twenty-foot-wide parcel bordered by the bicycle path and Wales Drive that leads to Narragansett Bay.
- Narrows peninsula, north of King Philip Avenue and Platt Street at the east end of Narrows Road, leading to Mount Hope Bay and the Kickemuit River.
- Platt Street extension, a 30- by 117-foot parcel on the west side of King Philip Avenue and just south of Platt Street, leading to Mount Hope Bay.
- King Philip Avenue, a 50- by 129-foot strip leading to Mount Hope Bay.

Bradford Street Right-of-Way Abandoned

From the earliest time, the terminus of all east-west streets in the village center was Bristol Harbor. The 1895 map shows a narrow sliver of land extending to the shore at the bottom of Bradford Street between the wharves of the Namquit Mills and the Wardwell Lumber Company.

At a June 1903 session of the Bristol Town Council, a public meeting ensued to hear property abutters and owners on Bradford Street in regard to the opening of the foot of Bradford Street. Captain Robert N. Turner took the position that the council had no right to open part of the street and abandon part of it. He claimed that such action was against the terms of the deed of gift of the streets to the town. At the conclusion of the hearing, the council granted the petition.

The council's decision was that "the foot of Bradford Street has ceased to be useful to the public. It ought to go further and say that it has ceased to be useful because of the obstructions maintained by the Richmond Manufacturing Company, Mr. Wardwell and the town of Bristol." The result of the decision was to move the right-of-way farther north on Thames Street.

The Premier Thread building (now Stone Harbour Condominiums) was built on the footprint of the Namquit Mill, the mill wharf, the former Wardwell Lumber Company and right-of-way. Bradford Street ended at the front door of the Premier Thread (Coats-American) building, but the town's bicentennial map shows a right-of-way to the water just north of the building. This right-of-way is also shown on the National Register Bristol Waterfront Historic District Map, 1974 and 1978 revised edition.

Salvatore Rossi told this author that the existence of this right-of-way was known to, and acknowledged by, the owners of the Premier Thread property. Because the right-of-way passed through the company's parking lot, the gate to the parking lot was never closed or locked, thus allowing free access by the public. Regrettably, this knowledge was not widely disseminated to the public.

Fast forward to 2004. The Bristol Town Council abandoned the relocated Bradford Street right-of-way in favor of the Stone Harbour Condominium owners. As a trade-off, Stone Harbour has built a handsome, attractively landscaped boardwalk along the Bristol shore in front of the condominium complex connecting the Independence Park boardwalk with Thames Street Landing.

The newly constructed replica of the circa 1840 mill cupola is being lifted into place on Wednesday, May 11, 2005.

Chapter Ten
The New Look

As much as old-time Bristolians detest change in the look and feel of the town's traditional institutions, time marches on and changes occur—for the better or for the worse, only the future will tell.

Historic Distract Blights

In the autumn of 2005, the Bristol Town Council passed a redevelopment plan for the historic downtown that gave the town authority to take action, including seizure by eminent domain, to compel owners of blighted property to take steps to clean up their properties within a certain time frame. Almost one year later, three of the four properties cited have made significant efforts to clean up and rehabilitate, and a fourth faces an uncertain future.

The so-called third oldest house on State Street, behind the former Brunelli plumbing building, faced an uncertain future. The owner claims the dilapidated two-and-a-half-story Federal-style home is beyond repair; the owner seeks permission from the Bristol Zoning Board and the Historic District Commission to tear down the structure and build another house in its place.

As of October 2007, the Bristol Historic District Commission granted permission to historic property developer James Towers for the house's teardown. In its place, Towers plans a new structure in the architectural style of the original for residences and commercial space.

Tuplin's Thames Street Garage was severely damaged by the 1938 hurricane. Rebuilt, the building took another devastating hit by the hurricane of 1954; since then the property has slowly deteriorated while being used primarily as a dead auto graveyard. The property consists of three separate buildings, two of which no longer have roofs.

The owner of the former garage, Louis DeAlmeida, who has owned the property for twenty years, hired Bristol architect Lombard Pozzi to draw plans for the circa 1930

The so-called third oldest house in Bristol as it appeared on October 15, 2006.

Tuplin's Thames Street Garage as it appeared in October 2006.

garage. The new plan calls for a mixed use of four residential units and two street-level retail spaces. In January 2006, DeAlmeida took his rehabilitation plan to the Historic District Commission; this was his first step in addressing the long-vacant parcel.

We read in the October 11, 2007 *Bristol Phoenix* of the demolition of the former Tuplin's garage at 382 Thames Street. The next step is for DeAlmeida to obtain a building permit for his planned multiuse construction to begin.

Colt-Andrews School Expansion and Pastime Theater Demolition

First there was the Colt School expansion plan that would have added an extension to the rear of the marble Colt Memorial building. That plan died after a public outcry and the promise of no approval by the Historic District Commission.

Then the Bristol-Warren School District Committee proposed a special election at which voters would have a chance to approve construction of a new school building on Naomi Street. Again, public outcry against the proposed location and the cost to hold a special election dashed that scheme.

Then came the Pastime Theater suggestion, and once again the public all but took up arms against the school committee and the Bristol Town Council. Few other issues have elicited as much passion as the Bristol Town Council's decision in November 2005 to seize the Pastime Theater and turn it over to the regional school district.

The Pastime Cinema in April 2006. All valuable or reusable contents of the theater have been removed and the building awaits demolition.

The razing of the 1930s Art Deco theater began on September 15, 2006.

This October 15, 2006 photo shows the vacant theater footprint and the formerly hidden east side of the Andrews School.

In this architect's rendering, we see the Andrews School with the proposed addition on the east (right); this view is from Bradford Street. *Courtesy of the* Bristol Phoenix.

The Town of Bristol had loaned $350,000 to the Bristol Pastime Theater Foundation, a group that had planned a rehabilitation of the 1934 Art Deco–style movie house as a venue for live stage presentations. With donations for rehabilitating the building failing, the town council decided to call in its note. After a few additional months of wrangling, the title to the building was turned over to the regional school committee, which promised to repay the town for the cost of demolition.

It took years to decide the theater's fate, but only days to bring it crashing down. A fixture on Bradford Street for almost six decades, bringing entertainment to Bristolians and visitors from neighboring towns, was sacrificed to make way for an addition to the Andrews School building next door. The demolition began on September 15, 2006, and by the end of the month the building was down, rubble was carted away and all that remained were the neat foundation walls and the cellar hole.

Rogers Library Expansion

The original plan for enlarging the Rogers Library called for the rehab of the two-story (formerly three-story[9]) furniture store building next door and the attachment of the two buildings with a covered alcove. Plans for the cosmetically rehabbed building ran into problems with the zoning board of review. Though Bristol zoning ordinances forbid the construction of buildings taller than 35 feet, the planned addition would rise to 33.16 feet on its Hope Street side and 41.16 feet on its Thames Street side. Since building elevations are averaged, the building's overall height needed a 3-foot variance to exempt it from the 35-foot requirement.

Finally, after more than five years of committee wrangling, architectural arm twisting and difficult fundraising, plans to demolish the Parella family's former Bristol Furniture store cleared the town council when the $193,500 cost to do the job was approved. The demolition was completed mid-November 2006. The approved bid was submitted by Aquidneck Construction of Portsmouth, the same firm that was currently pulling down the Pastime Theater on Bradford Street. Because the company's equipment was already in town, their bid came in at $45,500 under the second bidder.

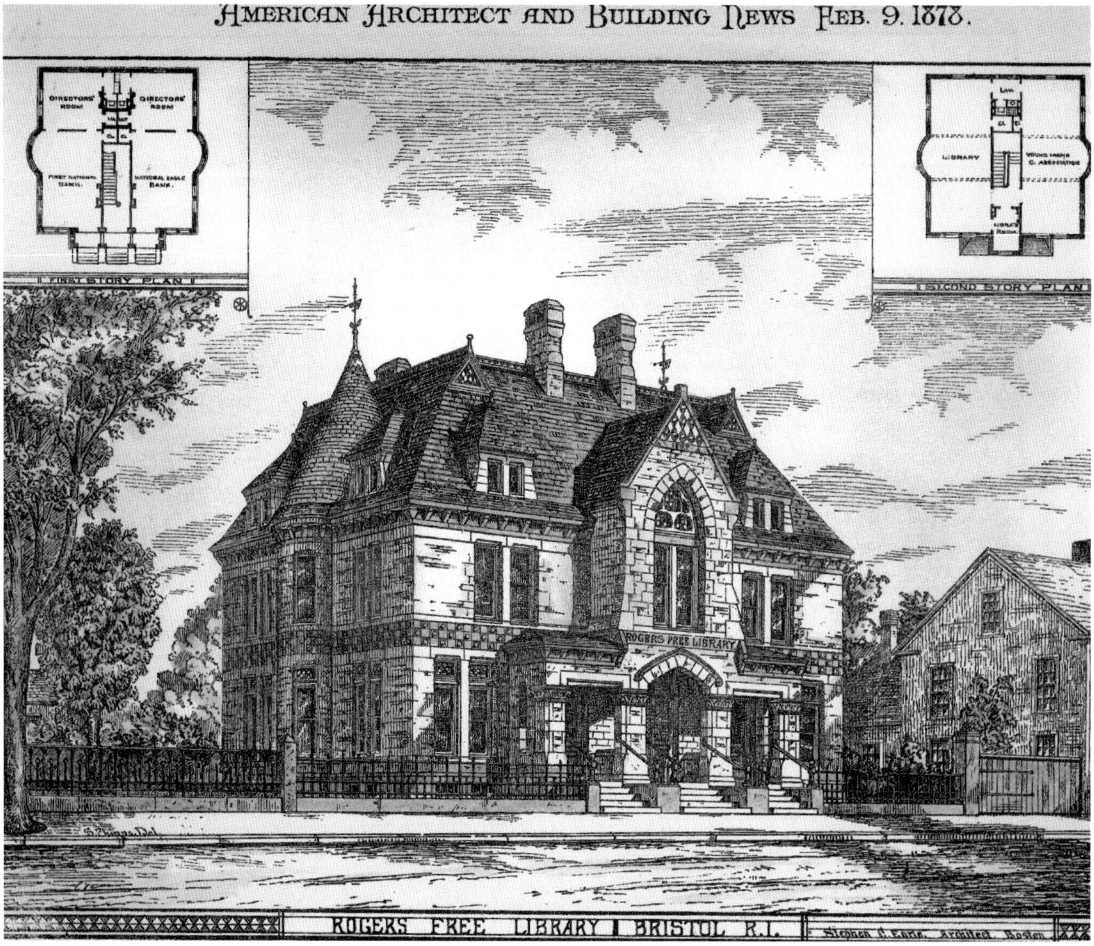

Stephen C. Earle's 1877 architectural drawing of Rogers Free Library as it appeared in the *American Architect and Building News*, February 9, 1878; notice the residential building to the north of the library.

Once the furniture store building was eliminated from the mix, the town dusted off a plan that had been shelved in 2001. While those plans had regained the interest of town officials, in March 2006, a similar but more conservative concept was drawn and presented by Bristol architect and preservation consultant Lombard Pozzi. This plan appears to be the "look" that all parties can agree on. Pozzi's model is a reflection of architectural elements prominent in the original Victorian-era brownstone library building.

On the financial side, David Swanson, who chairs the library building committee, said the overall projected cost will run between $9.5 and $10 million. Of that, about $8 million will go to construction costs. Funding from the state is expected to be $3.9 million. A May 2007 financial report brought joy to all concerned citizens with the news of a construction bid $2 million less than expected and the securing of $985,000 for a children's reading room.

With gala ceremonies, the long-awaited groundbreaking took place on Friday, May 25, 2007.

In this circa 1910 postcard we see the original 1877 Romanesque Revival Rogers Free Library building. In 1956, the upper story of the building was destroyed by fire. To the north of the library is the three-story commercial Hasbrouck Building.

The Hasbrouck Building was reduced to two stories on January 7, 1929, by a disastrous fire. In this October 30, 2006 photo, the Parella family's former Bristol furniture store is being demolished to make way for the Rogers Library addition.

This February 2007 architect's sketch shows the complementary styling of the planned library addition. The library architect is Dana Newbrook of A.I. Designs, and Bristol historic architect Lombard Pozzi is the project consultant. *Courtesy of Rogers Library.*

The Belvedere Hotel Saga

The Belvedere Hotel on Hope Street and surrounding properties languished for a decade under former ownership, but plans have taken shape and proper permits have been obtained by the new owners. Renovation of the century-old hotel will soon be completed.

For over a decade, the landmark Belvedere Hotel in Bristol's historic downtown faced an uncertain future, its fate locked in the hands of owners and developers who seemed unwilling or unable to raise the funds necessary to renovate it and several nearby properties on John Street. But the year 2006 brought new owners with ample funding and construction expertise. With new ownership and town and state approval, the long-awaited renovation of the old building and surrounding former Charles Falugo properties finally have a promising future. The following paragraphs chronicle the exhaustive and frustrating struggle.

Herreshoff

Around 1895, John Brown Herreshoff built the elegant one-hundred-room Belvedere Hotel on Hope Street in the center of the bustling business district for the convenience of wealthy clients who came to town to watch the construction and take delivery of their yachts.

This circa 1930 postcard image shows the Hotel Belvedere in happier days. The management offered first-class accommodations, gourmet dining and dancing in its enclosed rooftop pavilion.

Falugo

In 1955, James St. Angelo and his wife Harriet bought the hotel and renamed it the Harriet Bradford Inn, using her maiden name. In the late 1950s, the deteriorating red brick hotel was purchased by the Charles Falugo family. Over the next few decades the hotel lost its well-to-do clientele and became home to low-income families and some of Bristol's unsavory denizens.

After several warnings to the Falugos concerning unpaid real estate taxes, which had risen to $70,000, the town seized the property and offered it at a tax sale. In October 1995, a group of Bristol and Chicago investors acquired the tax title to the hotel and other portions of the downtown properties owned by the Falugos in that same Hope and John Street block.

Barrows

Eventually, in 1997, the property came into the hands of Ted Barrows, who planned to transform the old inn into sixteen two- or three-bedroom condominiums. Project developers, architects and engineers—Newport Collaborative Architects, Fuss and O'Neil—continued to frustrate the Bristol Planning Board for failing to submit or resubmit revised plans for the rehabilitation of the 101-year-old building.

State Superior Court Judge Michael Silverstein denied a request by Joseph Brito Sr. (an investor associated with Barrows) for a restraining order that would have halted

Stripped of its elegance, the empty hotel is seen in this April 2006 photo just prior to its rehabilitation.

the planning board proceedings. According to Assistant Town Solicitor S. Paul Ryan, the ruling meant the planning board could make a decision on the preliminary plan, but the town could not officially record any decision until the matter of who truly owned the property was resolved in court.

Ted Barrows espoused great plans to restore the place to its former glory. At a zoning board meeting in January 2003, he requested a one-year extension on the zoning variance that would allow for the restoration of rooms, including a sun parlor and ballroom on the building's roof. The variance originally granted in December of 1999 had expired by January 2003. Barrows, through his attorney John Rego, said his plans to reopen the building as a hotel were scrapped in favor of renovating the dilapidated structure into fifteen luxury condominiums.

"I hope this is the last time you come before this board for anything for the hotel," said zoning board Chairman Charles Alexandre.

Belvedere Developers LLC/Barrows

At the same time, there was the question of the liquor license assigned to the site. Board members were concerned about the yet-to-be-announced tenants for the pair of retail spaces fronting Hope Street. Anthony Murgo said he did not want to see another bar, similar to the raucous one in the old Harriet Bradford. William Hubbard of Center Development Corporation, one of the project's developers, said there were

In this architect's rendering we are granted a view of the renewed Hotel Belvedere with its new fully enclosed dining and dancing pavilion, from which patrons will have spectacular views of Bristol Harbor. *Courtesy of Newport Collaborative Architects.*

currently no plans to use the property's liquor license, but he stopped short of saying the license would never be used.

In December 2003, a question arose as to who actually owned the property. James Mullen, attorney for Belvedere Development heading up the rehabilitation of the blighted property, said, "Belvedere Developers LLC are the owners right now." With this latest snag in the project's progress, developers had no chance of breaking ground by the end of the year, as they had originally planned. At that point, seven years had elapsed since the purchase and planned development began.

Brito

Mr. Joseph Brito claimed his right to first refusal on the Belvedere property. He argued that right was triggered when a purchase and sale agreement was recorded early in 2003 between Belvedere Developers and Center Development Corporation of New York. Ted Barrows refuted that claim, stating that Center Development only was buying shares in the development and was not actually purchasing the property.

In August 2005, after nine years of work, plot changes and seemingly endless twists and turns, the Hope Street property was soon to find itself on the auction block.

The Center Development Corporation, which held a substantial mortgage on the property owned by Ted Barrows and his Belvedere Developers LLC, planned a foreclosure sale for September to recoup $2.3 million owed by Barrows and his partners. The foreclosure sale was scheduled because Barrow's group failed to pay off the mortgage by the July 28 deadline.

The auction, scheduled for September 13, was delayed when Barrows managed to argue before the Rhode Island Superior Court to postpone it. Barrows said his group was negotiating with a buyer for the property. He said he had hopes to wrap up the deal by the middle of November; he did not reveal the name of the interested party.

Town Government Takes a Stand

About the same time, the Bristol Town Council and the Bristol Planning Board, fed up by the continued delays in the rehabilitation of the blighted building, passed the town's new Downtown Redevelopment Plan. Among other things, the new plan gave the Belvedere's owners one year to begin rehabilitating the property or have it seized by eminent domain.

As the time for the delayed auction of the Belvedere property expired, Superior Court Judge Stephen Fortunato refused to delay the newly scheduled auction. While the auction was scheduled to get underway, Center Development attorney Jeffrey F. Brenner said that it could be canceled if Barrows filed for receivership before the 10:00 a.m. auction start time.

The Thames Street lot next door to Gillery's Tavern is cleared of collected clutter. In the back left of this photo is the west side of the closed Hotel Belvedere.

An architect's rendering of the planned town houses and street-level storefronts on the Thames Street lot between State and John Streets. The restored Hotel Belvedere is in the upper left. *Courtesy of Newport Collaborative Architects.*

Brenton Realty Investments, LLC

The complex's new owners, Brenton Realty Investments, LLC, received the unanimous vote of the Bristol Planning Board for their preliminary plan for the Belvedere. At long last the condominium project was nudged along to a happy conclusion as renovation began in earnest.

The Newport-based developer, Mr. John Roiter, purchased the Russell Warren–designed 15 John Street apartment building. Roiter also plans a new condominium and commercial building at the southeast corner of State and Thames Streets on a long vacant lot next door to Gillery's Tavern. Plans were submitted and approved by the town's building and zoning commissions; a spring groundbreaking was planned. As of mid-June 2007, no visible action had yet begun.

However, as of late October 2007 the building is swathed in a web of steel scaffolding, the interior gutted, walls reinforced and the rooftop pavilion nearly completed. A spring 2008 opening is expected.

The Bristol waterfront with the old J.T. O'Connell lumber and building supply yard next to the State Street Pier, circa mid-1990s. Gilbert's Seafood is the building in right center foreground. *Courtesy of Newport Collaborative Architects.*

A circa 1906 advertisement for the Seth Paull Co. on the footprint of the Thames Street Landing development. Most of the buildings in this illustration still exist; they have been rehabilitated and are in use as residential and commercial units. *Courtesy of the* Bristol Phoenix.

Thames Street Renewal

The face of Thames Street has returned to the way it looked at the turn of the twentieth century. The entire footprint of waterfront property, from the former J.T. O'Connell and Gilbert's Seafood properties north to the south end of the Premier Thread property, is now developed as Thames Street Landing, an upscale commercial and residential enterprise by a trio of businessmen, including Bristol resident Lloyd Adams.

The casual historian thumbing through many of the old Bristol pictorials extant will see these properties as a collection of five ramshackled buildings on 1.7 acres. The area contained a lumberyard, wharves, a bank and warehouses built as early as 1797. Formerly known as DeWolf Wharf, the area was, for decades, the center of Thames Street commerce and trade. Mr. Adams said the goal of he and his partners is to restore the old-time flavor to the property—bring back its original character. All five buildings will be restored, and an additional three new ones will be built.

Circa 1818, James DeWolf Warehouse: Two-story, 6,874-square-foot stone building is renovated and used for retail space, a restaurant, a banquet hall and service facilities.

Circa 1810, Byron Diman's Counting House: Two-story brick building now houses retail space and one apartment.

Circa 1800, William Taylor Store: The three-story wooden structure is now retail space and two apartments.

Circa 1797, Bank of Bristol Building: This one-story building was once three stories tall. It is now restored to its former height and now houses retail space, a lobby and eight hotel rooms.

Bank of Bristol addition: New construction restored the historic two-story structure for retail, service and four hotel units.

Former Coal and Lumber building: Reconstruction of a former building that once stood on this spot. The three-story building, made of wood and concrete, is now retail space and twelve hotel units.

Former Thames Street building: Reconstruction of a former building that once stood on this spot. Three-story building made of wood and brick, houses retail and office space, as well as two apartment units.

Wholesale seafood building: Once housed Gilbert's Seafood, was built in 1940. The original structure with the addition of a roof deck is now the home of a 150-seat restaurant and pub.

New construction includes an observation office to oversee and manage rental units, parking and boat slips. Another new building at the edge of the harbor is an old-fashioned ice cream parlor with thirty-two seats.

The abandoned Wardwell/J.T. O'Connell building supply store, consisting of the historic 1810 Byron Diman's Counting House (left) and 1800 William Taylor Store. *Courtesy of Newport Collaborative Architects.*

In this October 15, 2004 photo we see the fully restored (left to right) circa 1797 three-story brick Bank of Bristol building, the Byron Diman Counting House and the William Taylor Store.

Waterfront Condos and Marina

The Coats-American cotton factory buildings on Thames Street are long gone and now find new life as luxury waterfront condominiums. The property has morphed into eighty-five residential units and a private marina with thirty-four slips—twenty-four for small boats and ten for larger yachts. Public access to the water has increased with a landscaped boardwalk connecting Independence Park and Rockwell Park. The plan is to eventually extend the length of the waterfront boardwalk to the terminus of Thames Street at Constitution Street.

The 4.3-acre site at 345 Thames Street includes three adjoining buildings: a historic 1840 masonry building; the 1940 Premier Thread Company's red brick combination factory and office building with an Art Deco façade; and a 1960s prefabricated metal structure. These buildings were occupied by a manufacturing arm of the international thread maker Coats-American. When the thread company moved out, the Newport Collaborative Architects, working with Churchill & Banks, moved in to develop the site.

The historic 1840 Namquit Mill as seen from Bristol Harbor, circa 1875. *Courtesy of the* Bristol Phoenix.

Plans included maintaining the aesthetic Art Deco façade of the red brick building at the foot of Bradford Street, along with demolition of the prefabricated metal building at the western end of the property. On that newly opened land, an attractive multiunit brick town house now complements the look of the rest of the property.

Employees of the Namquit Mill gathered for this group photograph, circa 1900. *Courtesy of the* Bristol Phoenix.

In this December 18, 2004 photograph the partly restored Namquit Mill is viewed through rebar in place for the foundation of new construction, called Stone Harbour South.

By the time this photo was taken on May 11, 2005, the historic character of the stone and granite mill exterior was completed and the replica of the original copula bell tower was in place; the condominium sales office was open for business.

In this November 13, 2003 photo we can see much of the Premier Thread/Coats-American mill's 1940s Art Deco architectural embellishments have been removed for safekeeping during construction.

This mid-December 2003 photo shows the façade of the Premier Thread/Coats-American building held in place by a network of braces; the rest of the building is demolished.

As shown in this August 5, 2004 photo, the framing of the forty-six-unit Stone Harbour North is nearing completion.

This October 5, 2006 photo shows the Stone Harbour North complex fully landscaped and occupied by newcomers to Bristol, and some old-time Bristolians.

The Stone Harbour complex as seen from the wharf at Thames Street Landing, July 15, 2005. *Left to right*: Stone Harbour North, the Namquit Mill residences and Stone Harbour South.

The new face of Bristol Harbor as of July 15, 2005, as seen from the town's Rockwell Park dockage.

June 3, 1988, the author's 1810 Federal-style home on High Street.

Chapter Eleven

More Tales from an Old Seaport

The Mayor Vincent A. Cianci Jr. Tale[10]

Since he first gained the Providence mayor's office in 1975, the always colorful and controversial Mayor Vincent A. "Buddy" Cianci Jr. enjoyed being seen marching in Bristol on the Fourth of July and rubbing elbows with dignitaries and citizens at the chief marshal's post-parade reception.

In 1975, for his reception, Chief Marshal Dr. Manuel D. deSilva set up a large tent in the vacant lot next to his Bristol County Medical Center building. DeSilva said he sent out 986 invitations to state and local officials, personnel from the visiting ships and anyone who had donated more than five dollars to the celebration.

Mayor Cianci was not invited because he did not fit the criteria to receive an invitation. However, Cianci crashed the reception when his helicopter landed on the perimeter of the lot. Guests at the reception were less than delighted to see Cianci arrive; the downdraft from his helicopter props threw up billowing clouds of choking dust under the tent canopy.

In 1980, Cianci again crashed an event, this time the parade. Under Fourth of July Committee bylaws adopted in 1976, invitations to march are only issued to local, state and national officeholders; office seekers may not receive invitations to march. Parade Chairman Alan Guimond said, "The Committee strives to keep the parade from becoming a showplace for political campaigners."[11]

Guimond said that he and the rest of the committee were determined to keep Mayor Cianci out of the parade, but he admitted that he knew of no practical way to do it. The town council listened to Guimond's pleas concerning Cianci's appearance and unanimously moved to support the committee's efforts to bar "uninvited guests."

Mayor Cianci declared that despite the Parade Committee's decision to bar him, he would march in the Bristol parade. The Republican candidate for governor bristled. Cianci said his decision was prompted by a Bristol Police announcement that two policemen would be stationed at the muster area to keep out uninvited marchers and arrest anyone causing a disturbance.

"If they want to make an arrest," Cianci said, "they'll have to prove that they are right."

Just minutes before the parade started, Guimond asked to speak to Cianci, and standing in the middle of sunbaked Chestnut Street, he began whispering in the mayor's ear. Cianci laughed. The two men kidded each other and continued their conversation in the shade of a nearby tree.

"When I come back next year, I'll be governor and I'm going to march with the Matadors," said Cianci.

Guimond replied, "If you're governor next year, I don't think we'll have much problem. The governor is our guest."

The mayor's helicopter landed on the Colt High School athletic field. "They smuggled me in like the Trojan horse," he quipped. Cianci told Guimond, "It's been a pleasure doing business with you."

Guimond replied, smiling, "I'm not sure who was the businessor and who was the businessee."

Cianci proved that even without an invitation, he could still steal the show—and that he did. As he turned the corner of Chestnut Street onto Hope, the crowd, more than a dozen deep in places, began to cheer.

In 1983, the mayor defiantly marched in the parade despite being indicted for assaulting Bristol contractor Raymond DeLeo, whose high-walled and gated house at 2 High Street (Charles Rockwell's Rockledge) is prominently on the parade route.

Two police officers were posted outside DeLeo's home as a precaution, but Cianci marched by, seeming not to notice the party of celebrants on the front yard.

The following year, in 1984, after Cianci was convicted of the assault, he didn't show up at the parade. But when a clown clad in a striped prison uniform and carrying a ball and chain passed through downtown Bristol, a gaggle of hecklers began chanting, "Bud-dee! Bud-dee!"

In 1991, Cianci behaved rudely. He was invited to march in the Eleventh Division (Heritage), but he refused to take his assigned place in the parade order. He insisted on marching ahead of the division marshal, Ilidio (Leo) Contente. In answer to chants of "Bud-dee's back," the mayor threw the thumbs up sign, tossed salutes and blew kisses. The mayor later said he was simply marching with his own units, which included a group of Providence mounted police. Parade Chairman Marvin Perry said, "Cianci is rude and he doesn't deserve to be invited back."

In 1992, Cianci was unsaddled. He got through that year's parade without incident. But, according to witnesses, while the mayor was rubbing elbows at a post-parade party at a Poppasquash Road home, he attempted to mount a horse that was part of the Providence Police mounted unit. The mayor was not astride the animal for long.

"No sooner was he in the saddle then he started to go over to one side," a witness said. "It was like slow motion. Next thing I knew he was on the ground." Providence Police moved in quickly to aid their fallen leader, whose only apparent injury was a bruised dignity.

In 1997, Cianci heartily cheered. He walked the route accompanied by what seemed to be a small army of Providence Police: an honor guard, row upon row of officers and patrolmen, an equestrian unit, the K-9 unit, police rescue boats on trailers and a bicycle patrol. Capering members of the police department's Special Response Team blasted appreciative spectators with showers from high-powered water rifles. There were so many Providence Police in Bristol that some viewers wondered who was protecting the capital city.

The mayor's comely blonde parade companion, Tracy Kennedy, seemed in danger several times of being bowled over by the scores of Cianci fans who darted onto Hope Street to hug Cianci, shake his hand and snap his picture.

In 1998, without fanfare, the mayor had sailed into Bristol aboard his yacht, the *Nicole*, and taken his place with the Providence Police detachment at the muster area. Cianci showed up at Chief Marshal Partington's Linden Place reception in casual yachting togs escorting his young blonde friend Miss Kennedy. At the reception, the mayor's uniformed Providence Police chauffer bodyguard was seen standing nearby.

In 1999, Cianci was uninvited from the parade. At the committee's July 29, 1998 wrap-up meeting, Frances O'Donnell reported that the Parade Subcommittee met on July 13, and agreed to bring two issues before the General Committee for a vote.

The first issue was in regard to Mayor Vincent Cianci and the Providence Police contingent. O'Donnell read a letter received from the director of bands for Cranston East High School that outlined the band's displeasure with the actions of the mayor and his Providence contingent. It was recommended at the parade meeting that Mr. Cianci not be invited to the 1999 parade. Gena Campbell made a motion, seconded by Diane Davis, that the committee not invite Mayor Cianci and the Providence contingent back to participate in the 1999 parade. The motion passed unanimously. O'Donnell said she would convey the committee's decision to the mayor.

At the February 10 meeting, Frances O'Donnell reported that she had contacted Mayor Cianci's office to notify him that the large Providence contingent would not be invited to return. She suggested that the mayor consider a float representing the City of Providence.

In 2000, a beaming Mayor Cianci, now indicted on federal charges of corruption, was met with round after round of roaring applause and cheers from start to finish of the parade while sitting high upon a white Providence Police horse. The mayor, appearing to be leading his own division, was followed by police officers on horseback, Providence Police officials—including Providence Police Chief Urbano Prignano Jr.—and the uniform division.

Cianci was met almost everywhere with shouts of "Hey, Buddy" and "We love you, Buddy." Because he had been absent from the 1999 parade, some clusters of his diehard supporters along the route chanted, "Bud-dee, Bud-dee, Bud-dee," as he passed.

Only rarely did someone shout a reference to Operation Plunder Dome, the federal corruption probe that was plaguing his administration.

In 2002, the crowd was expecting it to be bye-bye Buddy. After being convicted by a federal jury on a racketeering charge, the buzz around Bristol questioned if Cianci would show up in the parade. He did indeed! Cianci received an overwhelmingly warm welcome as he marched through the town's streets on the fourth. While a few people booed the mayor and called him a crook, cheers from supporters, countless high-fives and scores of hugs everywhere he went drowned them out.

As he walked the 2.6-mile route, many parents pushed their children to the center of the road to shake hands with the six-term mayor. At every lag in the parade people ran up to Cianci to have their photo taken with him, and others offered typical Bristol hospitality with ice water, cold soda and even hot dogs.

The heat didn't stop Cianci, but he did choose to walk the route rather than ride on a police horse as he had in previous parades.

While there seemed to be more thumbs up than thumbs down, there were a few people who jeered the mayor with uncomplimentary shouts of, "Shame on you," and "Mafia? Yes." Another man shouted, "Go to jail. You're a convict."

As the parade and the mayor's golf cart came to an uncomfortably long stop in front of 2 High Street, Stephen DeLeo and several of his Moses Brown School chums began to lament the racketeering conviction of Cianci, a Moses Brown alumnus. DeLeo and his friends sang a chorus of "For he's a RICO felon, for he's a RICO felon, for he's a RICO felon, which nobody can deny."

If the felony racketeering–convicted mayor heard any of these jeers, he did not let on. The mayor's civilian aid requested a nearby band begin to play to drown out the students' ribbing.

At the end of the parade, Cianci hopped into his waiting liveried Lincoln Town Car and silently left town, perhaps thinking of his return to Bristol on the Fourth of July after he completed his five years in prison.[12]

In 2003, newly elected Providence Mayor David Cicilline faced inevitable references to former Mayor Cianci who, at that date, was serving his sentence in the federal prison at Fort Dix. Cicilline was accompanied by a noticeably smaller contingent than his predecessor.

As of November 2007, former Mayor Cianci has completed his "time away" and returned to the city of Providence where, to the delight of his many admirers, he conducts a daily radio talk show.

Colonel Colt's Mercedes

From the *Bristol Phoenix* column "This & That from Here & There," as told to Roswell S. Bosworth by Carlton Pinheiro.

In the peaceful days before World War I, it was customary for the aristocratic families of Bristol to vacation in Europe during the summer. The Colts and the DeWolfs often took their automobiles and chauffeurs with them. Colonel Colt chose from his stable of a dozen cars a huge 42 horsepower 1912 Mercedes Touring car for his 1914 European summer sabbatical. This car was probably chosen because of its fine handling ability and its 34-gallon gasoline tank, which needed infrequent filling while on tour.

Colonel Colt's chauffeur, Floyd Heustis, who was married on June 4, 1914, was informed that he was to take the Mercedes to France on June 20th as part of the Colt advance party. The Colonel would depart on the 6th of July after he had enjoyed the Fourth of July Celebration. Heustis, reluctant to leave his bride, also was concerned with inability to speak French and to drive around Paris. Colt insisted that he leave early to "get the lay of the land" and be oriented to the country and its roads by the time the Colonel arrived.

On the passage over, the chauffeur became acquainted with some young Frenchmen who were of considerable help after he and the Mercedes arrived at LeHavre. They all drove to Paris where Heustis drove them about on errands thereby gaining a good knowledge of the city and a good smattering of the language. When the colonel arrived, a bilingual footman was engaged for the remainder of their stay.

When war broke out, the Mercedes and Colt party were in Aix-les-Mains in the south of France. The Colonel wanted to drive to Italy and leave for home with the car. The French government would not allow them to take the car out of the country and they had to drive north to Paris where the Mercedes was impounded for military use. The Colt party left the country immediately, upsetting Mrs. Heustis' plans to join her husband in the last week of the junket for a touring honeymoon.

Before the war's end, the Mercedes was returned by the French government to Bristol, given Rhode Island registration plate number 7941 [obviously this was at a time prior to Rhode Islanders' mania for low number license plates], *and remained the Colonel's favorite until his death in 1921. Each year thereafter until 1937, the Mercedes led the Fourth of July parade.*

In 1937, the Colonel's former secretary, who had acquired the car from the estate, sold it to Ralph F. Kinder, Bristol's well known antique auto enthusiast. Kinder had not yet become deeply involved in his auto collecting hobby, but wanted the Mercedes out of sentiment. Kinder had been employed at the Colt garages in his youth and although he had driven many of the Colonel's other cars, he had never had the opportunity to drive the magnificent Mercedes. One of Kinder's Automobile Association of America racing associates of the dirt track days, Ralph Pewsey of Providence, prevailed on him to sell the Mercedes and he complied. On Pewsey's death, it went to the Webster Knight collection in West Warwick. It remained there until the mid-1960s when Carlton J. Pinheiro had the opportunity to inspect it and sit behind the wheel. Pinheiro said of the experience,

Although not as powerful as Colonel Colt's Mercedes, this sporty 1910 Herreshoff auto car was popular, and several cruised the streets of Bristol. At the wheel in this promotional photograph is Charles Frederick Herreshoff (1880–1954).

its designer

"Its motor was silent then, but I could imagine the sound of its whirring chains and full throated cutout speeding down Hope Street as Ralph Kinder had described it so vividly to me many times."

After Knight's death, the Mercedes was sold to Scott Isquick of Ohio who still had it as late as 1980. Pinheiro said he was told that the Isquick Mercedes collection was damaged by fire in the 1970s but the Colt Mercedes escaped harm. Pinheiro mused about the Mercedes returning, some day, to Bristol on a sentimental journey, in a cloud of exhaust and the echo of its magnificent engine to take its honored place at the head of the Fourth of July parade.

Also in Europe during that summer of 1914 was Colonel Colt's brother-in-law, Francisco E. DeWolf, and his chauffeur, Marius F. Paulin. DeWolf, known locally by the affectionate nickname "Hungry Frank," although 72 years of age, was a fancier of fine European motor cars and had owned a pre-1900 French DeDion-Bouton and an early scarlet-colored Mors. DeWolf, a titled Austria-Hungarian, customarily sat on the front seat with his 26-year-old chauffeur. He always carried a four-tube French auto horn and before reaching a corner he would raise the horn to his lips and announce his arrival with a melodious blast. Pinheiro said Paulin presented him with this horn about 1960 and regaled him with the story of touring Europe in 1914 in a new Renault Landaulet.

On a drive to Switzerland, while passing through Germany where there was a great deal of tension that summer, DeWolf devilishly pointed the horn at some peasants at the side of the road. Some miles ahead, alerted officials stopped the Renault and after searching the men and the car, finally allowed them to proceed, they were satisfied that the "gun" was harmless, although from a speeding car it did look like an old-fashioned pistol.

Upon returning to France at the war's outbreak, the Renault, like the Mercedes, was commandeered by the French government. This was done so quickly that Paulin didn't have the opportunity to gather his tool collection from the car. Although he was French by birth, he held this "tool theft" against France for almost a half century after the event. The Renault was used to carry French officers and men to the first battle of the Marne and was destroyed during the war or was confused with the many Paris Renault taxicabs, which were also commandeered for the battle.

Pinheiro said the only souvenirs of that historic trip are the horn, "which I often tooted in the Antique Car Division of past Fourth of July parades, a beautiful French lion radiator cap which now rests on my library shelf, Paulin's duster and goggles, and of course, Colonel Colt's Mercedes."

A Century of Storms

Distinguished Bristol architect and author George Locke Howe, writing in the 1967 edition of the annual *Rhode Island Year Book*, recounted the destruction heaped upon the town when the ocean occasionally roars up into the harbor during the September gales. These storms have drowned many a homebound sailor in sight of St. Michael's belfry.

The winter of 1779–1780 was the coldest in memory. The people of Bristol suffered more than any other inhabitants of the State. The entire supply of fire wood was exhausted, and the Legislature was forced to come to the relief of the town with a grant of fuel from the public stores. Wood sold in most parts of the State for twenty dollars a cord. Provisions also failed. Corn sold for four silver dollars a bushel, and potatoes for two silver dollars. For six weeks the bay was frozen from shore to shore. The ice extended out to sea as far as the eye could see.

The gale of 1815 drove William DeWolf's brig Juno, *160 tons, upwater from her wharf taking the sloop* Toadfish *with her. Together they hurdled the wharf of Deacon Royal Diman, and brought up against Captain Sam Wardwell's new brig sending her to the bottom. The buoys in the harbor were all uprooted. The south end of Thames Street was entirely washed away, the whole length of Constitution to Burton Streets. Four Poppasquash boys were drowned crossing the sluice of the old windmill at Windmill Point.*

The very next year, 1816, was long known as "1800 and freeze-to-death." Summer never came that year because of the eruption of the Pacific volcano Krackalowa. A severe blizzard struck in June, ice storms coated the trees in July; birds dropped frozen from the air; the corn crop failed, and farmers perished in snowdrifts.

The gale of 1869, a two-day September tempest, sank every ship in the harbor, uprooted 197 elms, toppled the Baptist steeple (yet to be replaced), and caused general havoc throughout the town.

In the tropical storm of 1938 the Methodist Church [steeple], *which since 1856 had soared into the sky on State Street, keeled over, skewering its steeple into the roof above the pulpit. The hurricane struck without warning with all her force, on the afternoon of September 21. The town was very fortunate in not sustaining any loss of life; however, the destruction of property was estimated at hundreds of thousands of dollars. The waters surrounding Bristol rose to an average height of 18 feet above low tide level, carrying with it many waterfront buildings and vessels. When the waters receded, tons of debris littered the shoreline and Thames and Hope Streets. Boats, large and small, were found tumbled on one another and resting on front and back lawns.*

Two of the town's largest industries, Collins and Aikman Corporation and Herreshoff Manufacturing Company, as well as many smaller businesses suffered heavy losses; the Bristol Yacht Club was a total loss. The spars and buoys from the Coast Guard Depot Dock smashed into the boat yard utterly destroying it. The empty tanks of the gas company were swept up to the Mill Gut on a fourteen-foot tidal wave. Octave LeClair's twenty-footer, the Go On, *rode over the seawall belonging to Isoline Barns to land with her stern cradled on the Barns' piazza.*

Hurricane Carol struck with devastating force on August 31, 1954. The rebuilt waterfront was again smashed to kindling. The harbor water, pushed on the in-coming tide flooded into Silver Creek. Thames, Hope, and Washington Streets, all under water, looked to be a lake.

The Lobster Pot Restaurant at Walker's Cove, rebuilt after the 1938 storm, took a direct hit. The heavy seas pounded the building tearing out the walls and floors. Tasca

Results of the 1938 hurricane made the Mount Hope diner's parking lot look like an auto graveyard.

DINER

Ford Sales and the Newport Creamery [where the Sip & Dip and the Top Sider are now located], *were damaged so badly that they never rebuilt in Bristol. All of Tasca's new car inventory was ruined; some autos floated to upper Washington Street. At the junction of Hope and Thames Street Ascoli's Service Station, Beretto's Service Station, and the Mount Hope Diner suffered heavy damage.*

The aftermath of both the 1938 and 1954 storms left many homes flooded or damaged by uprooted trees. Trees were pulled from the ground by the wind that was estimated to have attained a velocity exceeding 100 miles an hour. The town was without water, electric and gas for several days.

Mother Nature having almost frozen the town into submission the year before let loose with a barrage of powerful storms during the winter, culminating in the Blizzard of '78.

Earlier winter storms had left the town reeling, but the blizzard that struck on February 4, 1978 would prove to be the worst to this state since records were kept. For a week, little moved in or out of town; an experience most remembered for their lifetime. For some it was a harrowing time, but many have fond memories of a week spent close to home.

General Ambrose E. Burnside and Private Edward Anthony Jr.

From the *Bristol Phoenix* column "This & That from Here & There," by Roswell S. Bosworth.

Rhode Island furnished the only officer of the first rank, from New England, in the Civil War—Ambrose Everts Burnside.

Burnside was born in Liberty, Indiana, in May 23, 1824. In 1852 he married Mary Richmond Bishop in Providence. While serving as a first lieutenant of the Third Artillery at Fort Adams in Newport, during the Mexican War, Burnside was impressed with the need for more effective carbines. After much study he invented the breech-loading rifle which bore his mane. As a result, he resigned his commission to establish his firearms manufacturing company in Bristol. His factory in Bristol was not successful. However, when the Civil War broke out the Burnside Rifle Company, at the time in Providence, made 600,000 rifles for the Federal Government.

In 1861 Burnside was commissioned Colonel, in command of the 1st Regiment Rhode Island Detached Militia, and commanded a brigade at Bull Run. As Brigadier General he organized and commanded the celebrated Burnside Expedition to North Carolina. General Burnside took command of the Ninth Army Corps in 1862, and in November assumed command of the Army of the Potomac, numbering 225,000 men. He relinquished this command in January 1863, and after a brief rest at his home in Providence, took command of the Department of the Ohio.

Burnside resigned his commission in April 1865, and while a resident of Bristol was elected Governor of Rhode Island in 1866, and reelected in 1867 and 1868. In 1870 he was the medium of communication between the German and French lines, in and

General Ambrose Everts Burnside.

around Paris, in the interests of reconciliation. He was elected United States Senator in 1874, and reelected in 1880. Certainly, when he died in 1881, he had lived a full life.

Regardless of the glowing resume of offices held, Burnside was a bungler, and possibly the most inept and luckless commanding officer ever to command American armed forces.

There is no one like a retired hero, or an assumed hero, to inspire community pride. Bristol had two: Ambrose E. Burnside and Edward Anthony, Jr. For more than three-quarters of a century, they worked around the calendar to prepare the town's most glorious celebration of the nation's independence.

By the time General Burnside died in 1881, he had made the Bristol Fourth of July celebration famous. He imported orators from New York and Washington, where he sat as Senator from Rhode Island. He sent to Boston for fireworks. In 1876, the centenary of Independence, he got the Navy to order a man-of-war to the harbor; the steam sloop Juniata. *Yachts and excursion steamers came from all over Narragansett Bay to share in the celebration.*

In the parade, the General, as Chief Marshal, rode his Civil War charger Old Dick. A hundred sailors from the visiting ship marched behind the Bristol Train of Artillery band, and the town sergeant carried a standard which Nathaniel Byfield, one of the original proprietors in 1681, had presented to the town in 1724. That night a grand fusillade of fireworks lit the Common as bright as high noon.

Ed Anthony served on the Fourth of July Committee from 1864, with the Civil War still raging, until 1914, when he died lifting a rock that was too heavy for his heart. He was committee chairman from 1884, three years after General Burnside went to his reward, until that fatal year.

Anthony, who alternated with, and then succeeded, the General in command of the celebration, had been the General's "scout"—or, as he would now be known, his body guard—during the Civil War. Ed claimed that he had once been chased through a peach orchard in Georgia by a whole regiment of Rebels, and escaped them by hiding under a porch where Robert E. Lee was holding a council of war.

He lived with his sister Medora in a white house at the turn in the old Back Road—now Metacom Avenue—near the intersection of Griswold Avenue. Neither Ed nor Medora ever married. We learn from the writings of George Howe that it was told that a legacy from Captain Jim DeWolf, who died in 1837 kept the brother and sister alive, long after the DeWolf children had squandered their inheritance.

Each spring, Ed was the first in town to get his onion sets into the ground. Winter and summer he wore the same blue peacoat, with a black string tie and dirty roll-collar shirt. He explained the heavy coat kept out the cold in winter and the heat in summer. He never walked, but always dog-trotted, even on the mile-and-a-half trip from his house to the Town Hall. Each year, still at a trot, he carried a Christmas tree down to St. Michael's Sunday School. He never knocked on a door, but announced himself by an Indian war-whoop from outside. He loved lemon-balls, and the bigger the better. Once on the Fourth the Committee had one specially boiled for him, big as a fist.

He was a great marksman. He built a target of white quartz behind his house, rowing the stones over from Mount Hope. He practiced marksmanship with a ship's cannon. If the balls fell into the water, he retrieved them in his skiff; but this became costly, for he could not find every one. Thereafter, he used rocks for ammunition. Each summer he gave a shoot for the Train of Artillery, fifty muskets strong. He and Willy B. DeWolf, Captain Jim's grandson from The Mount, once with telescopic rifles, strung up two ducks each with one bullet, by waiting for the birds to get in range and then firing at just the right instant to send the bullets through all four heads, at a distance of three hundred yards.

Along his fence line Ed set tall poles, each braced in a cairn of white stones and topped by a cartwheel. He knew that the fishhawks would build their nest on the wheels

Edward Anthony Jr.

at the beginning of spring. Every spring for generations Bristol welcomed spring not by the calendar, but the day when George Fish, the scoutmaster, reported the first fishhawk on Ed Anthony's cartwheels, or on the tall trees in Tanyard Woods nearby the sewage treatment plant. In 1967, the great birds came to town on Friday, March 31, a week later than their usual return. That year, everyone had a late spring.

Bristol's Fourth and the Strongman

Mr. Bald Eagle has again spread his wings over the old town; Fourth of July has returned to Bristol; it's the town's secular holyday.

Old Glory snaps smartly in a freshening breeze playing off the harbor. Red, white and blue are the dominant colors; flags, bunting and streamers are everywhere. Boys from the various neighborhoods meet at the old Wood Street dump to construct a tower with discarded railroad ties and tar-soaked barrels for the ritual conflagration on the "Night Before." The continuous snapping of firecrackers, the screech-bang of rockets and the sputter of Roman candles filling the sky with balls of yellow, orange and red fire make each sleepless night everlasting.

For several evenings before the Fourth, band music fills the air from the bandstand, our "Temple of Music," in the geographic center of the common. The park is always festooned with gaily colored Japanese lanterns that trail down the four walkways from the forest of elm tree branches to its outermost corners, casting a festive glow over the whole place.

Such were the celebrations during the early 1900s.

One July, not too long ago, a Bristol acquaintance told me a story that his father told him of a particular celebration of some seventy-five years earlier.

Dad decided it was time to share some memories of past Fourths—some things he'd saved, "Get a couple of sodas, it's hot in the attic." It was a long time since I had last climbed the narrow stairs to the stuffy attic of Dad's 200-year old High Street Federal.

"There she is," he said, gesturing with a sweep of his arm and open palm, fingers pointing to the old paper-board and tin-veneered casket-domed trunk secured with crumbling leather straps and rusty hasps. "My chest of Fourth of July treasures," I detected a slight catch in his voice as he hesitated, and then spoke the word, "… memories."

"The celebrations haven't changed much since I was a boy," he said as he popped an icy-cold soda can, "the game's the same, only the players have changed." He began rummaging through the trunk's contents, removing and setting aside posters, postcards, and scrapbooks of clippings; he spoke lovingly of the celebrations of fifty or more years ago, about his sister, Aunt Sarah, and his folks, my grandparents. "Here's the ribbon Sarah and I received for winning the three-legged race one Fourth."

Dad said when he was a boy, to go downtown to watch the big parade was like going to church. His Mom got him and Aunt Sarah all slicked up in their best clothes;

he in white shirt with red bow tie, Sunday knickers and spit shined shoes; she in her best ruffled summer dress with pink-sash, long black stockings and a red ribbon in her hair. They carried small American flags on sticks and waved them furiously trying to catch the attention of the Boy Scout color guard, or a town celebrity, or when they spied a family friend among the ranks of marchers.

Grandfather, tall, under his skimmer, sported his best vest draped with a heavy-gold watch chain and jeweled fraternal fob that flashed ruby in the sun. Only occasionally he tugged at his high-starched collar, but habitually smoothed his large black mustache with a cane-superior air, as he peered over pinch-nez spectacles.

Grandmother, I was told, walked straight and proud in her layers of best summer-linens, with the same practiced imperial bearing as the town's high-born Grande Ladies who rode in the parade in covered carriages, with liveried drivers, drawn by well-groomed matched pairs of chestnut mares with ribbons of the national colors braided into their manes and tails.

The family always watched the procession from father's favorite viewing spot—in front of the post office, across the street from the Hotel Belvedere. This vantage point, on the elevated sidewalk, afforded not only an excellent view of the procession, but also glimpses of wealthy yachtsmen on the Belvedere's three balconies.

After the Grand Civic, Military, and Fireman's Parade passed the review, other Fourth of July activities for young and old centered on the Town Common. For longer than anyone can remember, there has been a carnival on Bristol Common for the Fourth of July. Games of team competition, vaudeville exhibitions of talent and unusual feats, and sideshows with wondrous displays of human oddities; all presented as part of the official Independence Day celebration. One particular presentation, an unequaled feat of strength presented on July 4, 1905, made the day memorable for my father; witnessed by him at age seven, it made an everlasting impression.

Finally, Dad removed from the old trunk a slightly-foxed, but otherwise amazingly well-preserved copy of the July 2, 1905 issue of the Bristol Phoenix*; secure, inside the centerfold of the newspaper, was a brightly colored, boldly-lettered and illustrated carnival poster: "Big July 4th, Rouge Bros. National Carnival, on The Midway, on Bristol Common After The Grand Parade. Rides. Games. Entertainment. See the world's strongest man, Captain Felix Kinderkraft* [Strongchild? Undoubtedly, his theatrical moniker]*, late of the Imperial German Army, perform amazing feats of physical strength and endurance. The heroic Captain Kinderkraft will attempt to support the weight of a self-propelled autocar with passengers on his unprotected and naked chest. Come one, come all." Fanciful drawings of the strongman in various poses illuminated the poster.*

"The strongman was in the Civic Division of the parade," Dad said, as he placed the poster on the growing pile of ephemera, "He rode in the back of an open automobile—presumably the one that was to run over him. He wore a German Army officers' uniform, his chest was covered with rows of colorful ribbons that supported gold and silver medals the size of Carson City Dollars; around his neck hung a large Iron Cross from a black and silver ribbon, and one of those silver crescent-shaped things that denote a person's rank. I was really impressed by his plumed-spiked helmet, from which he tossed off salutes to the crowd."

Next, we turned our attention to the newspaper. Under the front page announcement "Parade musters at 10 AM on Constitution Street, facing east, Chief Marshal Wallis E. Howe will begin the march at 10:30 AM sharp, and proceed to the Town Hall where Exercises will be held," and "Orders of the Day," we found the proclamation, "An Exhibit of Brute Strength by the World's Strongest Man on the Town Common after The Parade," an illustrated story about the man dominated a full eighth of the page.

Captain Kinderkraft had submitted to an interview by the newspaper's master of hyperbole, the so-called Scribe. "Upon arrival at Bristol, Monday, with his fellow troupers," the Scribe began his report, "Captain Felix Kinderkraft, the self-proclaimed 'King of the Muscles,' presented himself at our Bradford Street offices to place an advertisement to insure a great turnout of the curious to view his novel exhibition of brute strength. Recognizing the celebrity from carnival posters, we immediately seized upon the rare opportunity to interview the man.

"He is one of the most wonderful athletes that we have been permitted to meet. He seems to have discovered the secret of combining within himself muscular power and beauty of physique. By wise and judicious training, this man who is under 6 feet in stature, has succeeded in acquiring the faculty of developing powerful muscles. Kinderkraft is a student of Attila, a school of physical culture, which is highly successful in forming strong, harmonious, and well-muscled men out of weak and even sickly ones.

"The honorable Captain obliged the Phoenix*'s quick-sketch artist by removing his shirt and sitting for the drawing reproduced on this page. We encourage all who are able, to visit the booth set up for him on the common and witness a wholesome exhibition of male beauty and strength. This is his only Rhode Island appearance."*

Both Dad and I wondered if the endorsement was considered ethical reporting or was it paid for in the cost of the Kinderkraft's advertisement.

"We all witnessed that show," Dad said, as he continued his search in the trunk, "I'll tell you what I remember, while I keep looking for the next Phoenix*; that one has the Scribe's report on the celebration and the strongman's sideshow.*

"Well, with so much pre-show publicity, the common was mobbed for all three shows. After father paid the ten-cent admission, we walked inside the curtained perimeter of the side show tents. Kinderkraft's booth—what 'Karnie' folk today call a 'joint'—was a multicolored-striped tent, about 18-feet square, with pennants flying from the tops of the central and corner poles. The elevated stage appeared to be a platform formed by a mechanical extension attached to a low-gear wagon, like an oversized folding camper.

"We had all come to see a man crushed by an automobile. Sarah and I held hands, your grandmother held my left hand and your grandfather held Sarah's right hand as we tried to get close to the stage. Eventually, father hoisted me onto his shoulders for a better view. When from the darkness at the covered part of the stage the strongman came forward, he was wrapped top to toe in a rose-colored, silky looking, hooded-cloak with silver flames stitched on the shoulders, back and chest. With a dramatic flair he sweep off the cloak, it flew across the stage, to reveal a very muscled, and except for very abbreviated cotton shorts, a very naked man. I seem to remember the sound of

feminine gasps; I looked down at your grandmother who, to protect my little sister from the gratuitous display of masculine flesh, held her hand over Sarah's eyes; even though she could see nothing but the back-side of the woman in front of her.

"In the glare of the early afternoon sun, the strongman went through a series of poses to show off the development of the muscles of his neck, chest, back, biceps, thighs, and calves of his legs. He performed a series of muscle-rolling demonstrations; with his powerful fingers he tore in two as many as six packs of playing cards as if they were no more than a package of cigarette paper.

"Finally, an open touring car, the same one as we saw in the parade, chugged up. Kinderkraft, come down from the stage, mounted the car's running board, and with a gesture to us to follow, he rode the short distance to the arena prepared for the spectacle. This was the 'crushing' exercise we had all eagerly awaited. With showy theatrics, the strongman went to the center of the ring where a platform the width of the automobile's axle was arranged, unbalanced, on a large sawhorse. There, he rested on the ground on his hands and feet, his body facing upward; imagine his body shaped as an arch. On his knees and chest, assistants placed an apparatus in the form of a bridge made of large beams; now think of him as the pivot-point of a see-saw; the saw horse was removed, and the formerly unbalanced platform was placed—balanced—on the pivot. An assistant tilted one end of the platform to the ground as the automobile with three passengers for a total weight of more than a ton, moved slowly up the incline, and ran over the track of which Kinderkraft formed the living support. After the car passed over the part supported by Kinderkraft's body, the vehicle, through its own weight, caused the track to tilt to the opposite side, then it descended quickly to the ground. It was quite a show."

Just as Dad finished his story, he triumphantly pulled out the old newspaper he was searching for, "Here's that newspaper; let's see how the Scribe wrote-up the side show." We quickly searched the paper's eight pages for the expected banner headline; finding none, we looked more deliberately until we found the following: "Independence Day Celebrated. From all reports we have heard of the day, everything went off without a hitch. Chief Marshal Howe did his job well; the parade began and ended on schedule. Exercises at the Town Hall were laudable. The carnival and fireworks were entertaining. As we were invited guests to the celebration in Warren, we were out of town on the Fourth."

A Late Summer Clambake

An acquaintance who wishes to remain anonymous has allowed this author to relate the following tale, taken from the diary entry of a long deceased relative. This is his account of a delightful afternoon clambake on the Bristol shore.

Being the fortunate recipient of an invitation to a clam bake[13] *on the second Monday of September 1885, sponsored by the Ladies of the Episcopal Church for the youth of the parish, I feel compelled to record the circumstances of the day and of the epicurean delights encountered.*

Arriving at the steamboat landing, near DeWolf's Wharf, at the appointed time I spied already present, the Freeman family—the Bake Master, his wife and son who were hired for the day. Closely following came the carriages and buckboards filled with merry picnickers, then a small omnibus that had gathered up additional guests who could not have otherwise gotten here from the town's outer plantations.

Among the new arrivals were the Pickering brothers, Elliott and Joe; Noel "Buzzy" Chester and his sister June, and Miss Lizzie Ashford, the reputed "belle" of Bristol, although the title is sometimes disputed by admirers of other belles, who amiably concede the second place to Lizzie.

Mr. Freeman, who wanting to arrive at the site of the bake before the party to prepare the bake-pit, preferred the land route and left the wharf with his wagon of fresh clams, lobsters, corn, and potatoes after paying his respects to the bake's organizer.

While the crowd disembarked their respective conveyances and milled around the wharf awaiting the steam launch, now quickly approaching for the journey across our serene harbor to the little Poppasquash peninsula, I meditated upon how this place would have appeared two-hundred years earlier—Indian country.

Poppasquash, still referred to by many as Pappoose-squaw, affords endless discussion; in idle hours of picnicking or clam-baking thereon, as to whether the squaws and their babies were actually taken there for protection in absence of their sachems on occasions of hunting or battle. From the town view, the point of Poppasquash seems to lap over upon the most northerly point of Prudence Island, though the broad Narragansett Bay flows between.

With a population of some 5,400 souls, Bristol is such a peaceful little town—so much so, we have heard it called "dull." The rest of the town view from this spot is townward, and most handsome where the ancient wharves are most obscured by coasting schooners and yachts, and the attention thus diverted from the shanties and warehouses of Thames Street by the water to the elm tops of shady Hope Street, parallel above.

Seemingly reading my thoughts, an unknown launch-waiting companion said, "What a beautiful place to grow old in."

"No wonder people forget to die here," said another. I smiled, nodding, remembering the annals of unexpected longevity, the boast of Bristol for generations.

Whatever the depths of this subject, we shall leave them to be fathomed later. Our immediate concern is to happily consider only today's clam-bake in company with a blithe summer party, to some of whom the bake is wholly novel.

The Herreshoff steam launch supplied by the Neptune Boat Club is specious and comfortably accommodates us twenty-or-so revelers. The gaily striped canvas awning of yellow and green protects us from the scorching rays of the forenoon sun and the sooty smoke from the boat's coal-fired boiler; the colorful flapping pennants made a truly festive sight as we leisurely steamed across the tranquil harbor to our destination.

"What a salty-sea smell!" said June Chester, leaning forward across the port gunwale inhaling deeply, "and I'm sure that those bunches of algae that you call 'rockweed' are giving out volumes of iodine to-day."

"I thought that I caught a whiff from the fish-works on Prudence," prosaically observed her brother Noel.

"Buzzy, you dreadful boy!" scolded a chorus of eavesdroppers.

"The prettiest picture of rockweed is under a sail-cloth and over a bed of steaming clams," replied Noel, determined to be fully practical.

Steaming north for a few moments only, then sweeping to westward, we follow the curve that forms the head of the harbor. Coasting the east shore of Poppasquash to our picnic grove, I glimpse Willow Walk, the shore-road bordered with ancient trees of this kind, open between the rude framing of their knotty trunks and pale olive leafage is a succession of picturesque views. From our chugging conveyance the sky and sea are rivals in sapphire and turquoise tints and in the middle distance is the first green island—little Hog, then pretty Bristol—truly a gem in the distance, with its variety of roof and spire and lines of elm-shaded streets.

Our destination finally achieved, we disembark the launch. It being low tide, we tread with caution; holding hands for safety, across the sandy strand of Usher's Cove cautious not to stumble on a hidden stone. The entire breadth of Poppasquash being recently subdivided into cottage and villa lots from the boat landing at Usher's Cove to the Point by Levi DeWolf Perry, our bake takes place at the common ground provided by Mr. Perry as a public recreation area at the convergence of Perry and Shore Avenues.

We are welcomed by the Freemans who have a roaring fire heating rocks in preparation of receiving the fresh clams and rockweed.

Excitement reigns! My merry companions charge up the shore, jumping from rock to shore, and rock to rock, greeting and grouping, and separating and grouping anew, choosing their places to set their baskets crammed with sundry pastries and beverages, spread their carriage-rugs and Afghans, and a few who could not resist dashing down again to the water's edge to race with the rise and fall of the tide-waves, or dip their hands, or throw flat stones, edge on, so that they skip or rebound from the water.

"But the clams, Joey Pickering—where are the clams?" eagerly asks Elise Brenner, one of the strangers, desirous of witnessing the process of the "bake" from beginning to end.

"Presently," responds Noel Chester, tugging at his side of a huge basket of clams, the other supported by Samuel, son to the Bake Master who is to superintend the "mysteries" of the bake, "presently," he repeats, "clams for all."

"Oh my! How many?" asks Elise and Joe in a breath, as the pile was increased by renewed basketfuls. "Who will eat so many?"

"Guess you never got a clam appetite outdoors," observes the Bake Master's son, now engaged in piling the clams over the same rockweed that Lizzie had earlier likened to a lion's mane. "Besides," he adds, "your mind's a measuring the shells, which ain't eaten."

As I remember, the rockweed was covered with a sail-cloth. Mr. Freeman gave himself the task of watching, while his son stacked other baskets in which green corn was brought to be buried in the roast with the clams. The guests devoted themselves to the water and its sparkle, the beauty of sail near and far, the canvas of distant coasters beyond Chesawannoc or spread on lively yachts skimming the harbor's surface.

It fell to Robert Elliott to initiate Elise Brenner into the manner of eating clams. The fragrance from the now uncovered bivalves had for several minutes appealed to

The Herreshoff steam launch, the *Dido*. This was a popular sixty-foot launch in use at the turn of the century. *Period postcard.*

stomachs that were near hearts that knew no sentiment, and the company sat down at some rudely extemporized tables that were swiftly constructed of planking and supports brought along for the purpose by Mr. Freeman.

With steamed corn in-husks, potatoes in jackets, slices of brown bread, melted butter, and jugs of lemonade held in readiness, the clams were brought forth.

Robert, vigilant in his duty, cautioned Elise to forgo the nicety of a fork, "With fingers only, fingers to clams—see this way." Then he removed the delicious morsel from its couch of shell, dipped it in the butter, and conveyed it to his mouth, biting just short of the black neck-line that seems made for a finger-hold, without the least offense to delicacy.

"Why, that is real Indian, isn't it?" said Elise, smiling, but succeeding admirably in her first attempt.

There, ends my reverie of the meal, for I shall not shock the critic by portraying the feast at length. No man is fit to judge who has not shared the temptations presented to this party of hungry, happy youth. As they retreated from the table, the piles of shells would have been the occasion of remark to any but veterans.

As we passed the Bake Master, he drew himself up with an air of knowledge, addressed Elise and Joey, "What do you think of the quantity now, Miss?"

"I am almost ashamed of having eaten more than I ever did in my life," she said simply, to which Mr. Freeman laughed and seemed content at having presented another successful Bristol clam-bake.

Horse Chestnuts and Walker's Island

While walking down High Street to the harbor at Walker's Cove, the scent of salt and the snap of autumn are in the air. The invigorating salt air caresses my nostrils as the crisp coolness of the late afternoon reddens my cheeks.

I reflect, *Another Halloween is almost here*, as I kick horse chestnut shells aside. *The horse chestnut harvest is abundant this year. The kids don't collect them and play Kingers like we did when I was young. Too bad!*

The fruits of the town's great old horse chestnut trees litter the sidewalks and streets. The ground under every tree is thick with thorny green shells. Almost every one is split open, spilling out its ripe, mahogany-colored jewel. There they are, nature's bounty, free for the taking. Stooping, I pick up a pair of exceptionally large specimens. Holding them close to my face, I rub them together, releasing their woodsy aroma. The silky smooth and slightly shiny skin of the nut reminds me of the polished cabin accoutrements of an expensive sailing yacht. Foul tasting to humans, these nuts are tempting morsels that are stored for winter survival by squirrels and other burrowing creatures.

My walk half finished, I sit on the wall at the harbor's edge at Walker's Cove and watch the incoming tide lick the algae-blackened rocks on the shore. From this vantage point, between the Lobster Pot Restaurant and Ray Deleo's boat-launching ramp, I have a clear view of Walker's Island lying about one hundred yards into the crotch of the cove. The island, from this aspect, appears as a low row of randomly piled rocks. These rocks once formed the foundation of the fertile little arrow-shaped island. Alas, the poundings of too many nor'easters washed away most of its earth, thus losing its ability to support the few spindly pines and fir, tangles of prickly barberry and its crowning glory, an ancient seventy-five-foot-tall horse chestnut tree that flourished there.

August (Gus) Miller, the son of Bristol artist Oscar Miller, told me that when he was a boy, he and his crew of chums used Walker's Island as a hideaway—their island fort. That was long before Tony Nunes filled in a part of the cove and built his raised town houses and before the Pearsons and the Herreshoffs used the cove shore to store yachts on marine cradles; that was in the days when Tanyard Brook ran clear and clean into the cove and soft-shell clams were abundant.

At mean low tide the flats were navigable by foot to the island's shore. The clams, when disturbed, spat their briny liquor, revealing their whereabouts to the hungry boys who relished them steamed in a bed of seaweed, as the youth of today still do. When not working at one of the town's numerous dairy farms or boatyards, the boys' leisure time was spent harvesting clams from the flats around the east, north and south of the island and casting nets for skipjack off the island's west shore.

Over the length of three summers, during the first decade of the 1900s, Gus and his pals carried many armfuls of discarded boards of varying widths and lengths across the flats. With this lumber they constructed a rather cozy and weather-resistant clubhouse under the branches of that majestic horse chestnut tree. Many a long, hot summer day was spent building, repairing and enlarging the clubhouse. Countless evenings were spent telling stories around a bonfire of driftwood or eating steamed clams, skipjack and corn, or apples purloined from a nearby orchard.

But it was the horse chestnut tree that originally drew the boys to the island. That magnificent century-old tree was of such thick girth it took four boys with outstretched arms and locked hands to encircle it. Its lower branches drooped, yet turned up at the tips, its showy white flowers stood up as conical candles upon leaves of five to seven leaflets in a cluster. It was the fruit, that precious seed, which held the boys' rapt attention. They watched for that fruit, encased by a green, short-spine burred husk containing one or two large scarred brown seeds, to fall to germinate.

While clamming, seining and building their shanty clubhouse, the boys worked as a team. When the horse chestnuts began falling, it was each boy for himself. For every boy, the object of securing a horse chestnut seed of superior quality was the promise of owning the season's most winning Kinger. If no ideal nuts were on the ground, it was then a matter of shinnying up that old tree and crawling out onto the limbs where some promising specimens were still hanging.

Each boy had different ideas about the Kinger quality of horse chestnuts. They all agreed, however, that the nut has to be about four inches or so in circumference, with the soft, tan-colored spot as near to center as possible. A nut with these features has the qualities of a champion in the game of Kinger. Some boys used the nut as it is found, while others believed champion Kingers had to be nurtured by hardening. Hardening was accomplished by baking in the earth under the evening campfire or freezing overnight in the family icebox—each method an unscientific personal preference.

Gus said his favorite way to make a champion "twenty Kinger" was to use his dad's hand drill to make the hole through which he passed his rawhide tether. Some other boys also used drills, but most used a nail and a rock as a hammer. Preferences for

Walkers Island in Bristol Harbor, looking south from the foot of High Street. *Circa 1910 postcard.*

tethers varied from Gus's rawhide to shoelaces and hemp twine. In any case, it had to be strong, thin and able to support a hefty knot, and stand up without unraveling in the heat of battle.

According to Gus, the object of the game of Kinger was to crack your opponent's chestnut. This is how the game was played. Boys with stringed horse chestnuts challenged each other. As a matter of pride, a challenge was always accepted. Fingers were thrown for "firsties." The loser of the finger throw would hold his chestnut out at arm's length by the string and the other boy would take a whack at it with his chestnut—whacks were called shots. As long as the boy's shots landed on target, he continued taking shots until he missed; then it was the other boy's turn.

Scoring was simple, but because it was based on the honor of the boy, it was ripe for cheating. Every time a boy's chestnut cracked that of another boy, the winning chestnut was awarded one point. However, when a chestnut cracked one that had been previously awarded four points, the winning chestnut absorbed those four points plus one and became a five Kinger. The ultimate goal was to own a twenty Kinger; that was the king of Kingers.

Gus once owned a nineteen Kinger, but his nut had only cracked one chestnut. He said, "One late October Herbie Duponte was the champ of the neighborhood. Herbie had three Kingers battling at the same time and all three were twenty Kingers. I don't want to imply that Herbie was a cheat, but come to think of it, he always claimed to have a twenty Kinger in his pocket."

Chapter Twelve

Gleanings from a Century of the *Bristol Phoenix*

The most inclusive unofficial records of Bristol, Rhode Island's history are to be found in the pages of the *Bristol Phoenix*. Founded and published continuously since 1837, the *Phoenix*'s writers have recorded the most salient of events. After searching hundreds of copies of the newspaper spanning one hundred years, I have included the following gleanings here for another airing.

January 29, 1876. "Winter has suspended for a time at least. She has failed in her stock of snow intended for this market, and so sleighing business in this vicinity is dull. Those beautiful moonlight rides are postponed, and 'Zekiel must stay at home with Huyldah in the parlor. It is somewhat a confinement to youthful affections and yet it cannot be helped this season."

February 1876. "The annual meeting of the stockholders of the Providence, Warren, and Bristol Railroad was held on Monday afternoon last, at two o'clock at the company's office in Providence.

General A.E. Burnside of this town was nominated to fill the vacancy in the Board of Directors caused by the death of President Clifford."

March 4, 1876. "Captain Richard Magee had a hog slaughtered on Tuesday last that weighed when dressed, six hundred and twenty pounds. This is the fifth porker of his raising, killed within a year, the combined weight of which amounted to two thousand, four hundred and eighty pounds."

March 18, 1876. "The Mount Hope Farm containing about one hundred and eighty acres, was sold at public auction on Monday last by George H. Reynolds, Esq., at Mortgagee's sale. Col. S.P. Colt of this town was the purchaser, and the price paid, $10,650, is considered to be very low for such a valuable property."

APRIL 29, 1876. "A silver bowl was exhibited to us on Wednesday last that is supposed to be at least two hundred years old. It was brought to this town by Captain Simeon Potter, and was taken from a mission station at the time of the capture of the fort and mission of Oyapoc, French Guiana on or about the 4th of November 1744, Captain Potter commanded the ship *Prince Charles of Lorraine*, in the 'Old French War,' a privateer from this port that cruised among the islands to the leeward of Cayenne, South America."

MAY 6, 1876. "During the month of April there was but one death reported in this town, and that from a pulmonary disease of long standing, which is without parallel in the history of this town for the last half a century, and which shows the wonderful degree of health that prevailed."

SEPTEMBER 15, 1883. "The ceremonies of laying the cornerstone of the Burnside Memorial Building will take place on or about the 25th inst. It possibly may occur a day or two earlier or a day or two later. The postponement from day to day was made with the full expectation that President [Chester] Arthur will be present when the exercises take place."

SEPTEMBER 22, 1883. "The large two-story brick dwelling house on the south side of Union Street, between Hope and High Streets, known as the 'Noyes house,' and belonging to Miss Seraphine Noyes, formerly of this town, but who now resides in Detroit, Michigan, was destroyed by fire Saturday morning."

SEPTEMBER 29, 1883. "The exercises of laying the cornerstone of the Burnside Memorial Building took place on Tuesday last, President Arthur being present and assisting in the exercises. The president arrived here on board the revenue cutter *Samuel Dexter*, about 12 o'clock noon, mid the artillery salutes of the Bristol Train of Artillery, and the USS New Hampshire, and other vessels in port.

"The President and his party landed at the National Rubber Co's wharf, where they were received by His Excellency Governor Bourne, Col. S.P. Colt and Grand Marshal Samuel Norris, and in Col. Colt's landau drawn by four horses, with red, white and blue plumes, proceeded to the Colt mansion on Hope Street. Col. Norris escorted the President from the carriage up the marble pathway to the residence of Col. Colt.

"The procession was formed on High Street, right resting on Church. The procession moved down Church to Hope to Walley to High to Franklin to Hope to the memorial building. The Orator of the Day was the Honorable LeBaron B. Colt."

OCTOBER 6, 1883. "Mr. Nathanael G. Herreshoff has a large two-story dwelling house, with large piazza and cupola [Love Rocks], nearly completed on the south side of a continuation of Walley Street, west of Hope Street, which commands a fine and unobstructed view of the harbor, bay and neighboring island. Mr. John Slade is the builder."

October 20, 1883. "The fellow, who by mistake, sent his auburn-haired sweetheart instead of a bottle Dr. Bull's Cough Syrup a bottle of hair dye, wants to know the best way to commit suicide."

October 27, 1883. "The store opposite the railroad depot, occupied by Mr. William B. Gray, dealer in fruits and provisions, was broken into and an attempt made to set fire to the building, Thursday night. The scamp effected an entrance by breaking a window in the rear. Bunches of hay were carried in and set fire to, but fortunately after burning up the hay the fire went out. Incendiary fires have been fearfully frequent here, and extraordinary exertions should be made to ferret out the rascally 'fire bug.'"

January 7, 1888. "There were nine hundred and thirty-four arrivals of steam and sail vessels, exclusive of small craft, at this port during the year 1887, as follows: United States steamers, 2; steamers, 751; schooners, 75; sloops, 20; barges, 86. Total 934. The number of arrivals in 1886 was 1008; in 1885, 1015; in 1884, 994."

January 28, 1888. "Dr. Jerome B. Greene, whose residence is on Bradford Street in this town, and whose office is in Providence, was surgeon of the Fifth R.I. Artillery, during the war of the rebellion.

"Mr. William Troy, an old soldier of the Fifth, sustained wounds during the war for which he receives a pension, and recently he had occasion to consult his physician regarding his papers. He came to Providence to confer with Dr. Greene. Mr. Troy was badly afflicted with rheumatism and his old surgeon attended him professionally.

"The patient improved rapidly. He appreciated the doctor's services in a very substantial manner for he conveyed to Dr. Greene forty acres of land at Daytona, Volusca County, Florida. The deed was signed by Troy and his wife, acknowledged before Judge W.A. Philips, of Providence, and duly recorded. It is said the land can easily be transformed into a prolific orange grove. That was a good present."

February 25, 1888. "On Sunday last as Honorable W.T.C. Wardwell and family were driving home from church, Mr. Wardwell noticed that something was the matter with his horse, and stopping him alighted from the carriage, and with the aid of some one near, disengaged the animal from the vehicle. The horse walked about his length and dropped dead."

March 17, 1888. "The petition of Honorable W.T.C. Wardwell and others, of this town, was presented to the Legislature, Monday, for an act to incorporate the National India Rubber Company, which was referred to the Committee on Corporations. The capital stock of said corporation is not to exceed $500,000, to be fixed in amount from time to time by vote of the corporation or by its by-laws."

April 7, 1888. "The Herreshoff Manufacturing Co., of this town has just received a contract from the United States Government for the construction of a submarine torpedo boat at a cost of $82,750."

MAY 5, 1888. "The factories of the National India Rubber Company of this town, will be started up on Monday next. All the property of the old Company passed Thursday to the new, by deed, which was left on the afternoon of that day at the Town Clerk's office for record.

"In reorganization, $700,000 of common stock has been wiped out, and three-quarters of the $500,000 of indebtedness—on quarter of the remaining debt has been converted into stock of the new company.

"Wages will hereafter be paid promptly every two weeks. Col. Colt is to retain the Treasurership of the company for the present. At a meeting of the directors, Mr. I.F. Williams was elected Superintendent."

JUNE 9, 1888. "Strangers visiting Mount Hope are always charmed with the prospect from its summit. Although but a moderate elevation, it commands some of the most beautiful scenery to be found in New England. No wonder that the spot had strong attractions for the Indians, or that the most famous of their chieftains fixed his home in that neighborhood."

JULY 14, 1888. "The sailboat belonging to Mr. Leonard P. Sanford was stolen on Friday night of last week by two boys, James Thompson and Thomas Holk. The boys were arrested at Narragansett Pier, Saturday, and brought here by Sheriff Pearce."

NOVEMBER 17, 1888. "The republican celebration of the election of Harrison and Morton came off in this town Tuesday evening and proved a successful affair.

"The demonstration was under the auspices of the Bristol Republican Club, who were joined in the parade by a delegation of the Plumed Knights, the Red, White and Blue Battalion, and a Company from the First Regiment Boys in Blue, from Providence, and a Company of 'Belva Lockwood's' in burlesque female attire, including a live colored lad in a baby carriage that was wheeled over the entire route. The music was furnished by Reeves' American Band, the Slocum Post Fife and Drum Band of Providence."

JANUARY 1903. "It was fortunate for David Campbell, a veteran of the soldier's home, that he was discovered laying on the road on Chestnut Street, Bristol Neck, last night for he would no doubt have perished from exposure to the cold weather which prevailed last night. The man is afflicted with paralysis and has much difficulty in walking and he had fallen and was unable to rise. Mr. Thomas Brides assisted him to an electric car and accompanied him to town where he was turned over to police, who put him up for the night."

FEBRUARY 1903. "The train on the consolidated road, which left here at 9:15 a.m. Wednesday, collided with a car loaded with ice in the railroad yards at Warren, lifting the ends of both cars and giving the passengers, all from Bristol, quite a shaking up. The car loaded with ice, when being switched, took the wrong tracks."

FEBRUARY 1903. "Capt. John M. Connery, paymaster of the factory of the National India Rubber Company, sustained a severe cut on his chin last evening by a fall. He had been to Providence where he had teeth extracted, being under the influence of gas during the operation. After his return to Bristol, he seemed to be not fully recovered from the effects of the gas and fell when leaving the car at the depot. Seven stitches were required to close the wound."

MARCH 1903. "There was much surprise on both sides when the vote for fifth councilman was announced, as it was expected that F.L. Waldron would receive the largest majority of any of the candidates in the Democratic-Citizens ticket. He defeated Walter E. Munro by 34 votes.

"Elated with their victory, a group of democratic supporters put together an impromptu parade on election night, complete with marchers and a band, and visited both their allies and their opponents.

"After Mr. Cole's serenade the procession moved a short distance to the south where a serenade was given to John B. Herreshoff, in front of the latter's home. Mr. Herreshoff had been prominent in the citizens' movement to defeat the Franklin ticket and while the marchers were in front of his residence the band played 'Ain't dat a Shame.'"

APRIL 1903. "*Reliance*, the sixth yacht built by the Herreshoff Manufacturing Co., as a cup defender, was successfully launched Saturday evening from the south shop, whence all but one of the six have emerged to take their maiden dip in the harbor."

MAY 1, 1903. "Now that the town council at its last meeting decided that the town should pay only one third of the cost of making concrete sidewalks instead of one half, as had been done for some years, it is probably true that many property owners will wish that they had taken advantage of the town's more liberal terms in years past."

MAY 5, 1903. "The new depot of the New York, New Haven, and Hartford Railroad Company at the terminus of the tracks at the foot of Constitution Street, at the corner of Thames Street, was opened to the public Sunday and is greatly appreciated by those who live in the south part of town."

MAY 5, 1903. "The police of this town received word today from police headquarters in Worcester, Mass., that a woman named Mary Rourke had left her husband and five children in that city and was supposed to be in this vicinity doing housework. She is described as short in stature, with high forehead and some front teeth missing."

JUNE 1903. "Noteworthy improvements are soon to be made in front of Linden Place, the residence of Col. S.P. Colt, and when they are completed the changes will add much to the appearance of that prominent portion of Hope Street. In place of the stone wall on the north border of the estate, which is, now being torn down a yellow pressed brick wall will be erected; the wall will have massive posts, surmounted by carved brown stone urns."

JANUARY 1906. "Frank Fredericks, who was one of the quartet arrested last Thursday evening for drunkenness, complained to the police Saturday morning that he had been robbed of $125 and he told police he suspected the two women, whose fines he paid the day before, of being the thieves. Capt. J.H. Morrissey went to Providence in search of the accused parties, but could not locate them."

FEBRUARY 1906. "There are several club rooms in town where, it is alleged, young men are in the habit of congregating for no other purpose than to play poker and to shake dice. Parents have reported that their boys are in the habit of staying out all night and are coming home without any of their week's wages, the police are well aware that there are several "old timers" who make it a business to visit the club rooms of these boys and fleece them."

APRIL 1906. "The work of moving the buildings from the corner of Hope and Bradford Streets to make way for Colt Memorial School is progressing as rapidly as possible. The Collins block has already been moved to the Morris Brothers' lot on Bradford Street and the old historical Richmond house has been moved as far as High Street. This latter building will also probably reach its destination, of the Morris Brothers' property, in a few days. The work of removing buildings formerly occupied by the Reed furniture company will probably begin some time next week. They will be transferred to Patrick Hammill's lot, corner of Wood and Congregational Streets."

MAY 1906. "A large amount of statuary has arrived from France to be placed on the walls of the new bridge on Col. Colt's ocean drive on the west shore of Poppasquash. The statuary came to New York by steamer from France and was brought to Bristol by rail and carried by team to Col. Colt's farm there are 15 figures, all different subjects, five of them being bronze, somewhat larger than life size. These include the Venus of Milo, the Gladiator, Diana, child with a butterfly, etc. Ten of the statures are of stone, and include the Venus de Medici, children, wild boars, a large urn with heavy carved upright pillars, etc."

JUNE 1906. "Many elm trees about town show the ravages of the elm tree beetle. The trees on the Common show plainly the effect of this destructive insect."

JUNE 1906. "At a meeting of the Fourth of July Committee, it was voted to add another division to the parade to be known as the Automobile Division. The owners of machines are invited to participate in the parade."

JUNE 1906. "Work has begun this week in the construction of a depot for passengers at Bristol Highlands. It is a good sized structure and will be a great accommodation to the growing colony at this point on the road."

JULY 1906. "Henry Govrow, a Frenchman, residing on Thames Street while under the influence of liquor, Tuesday evening, used a mason's hammer in a reckless way about his house, smashing the door and window. The man's wife sent for Chief of Police Hoard Wednesday morning and Govrow was taken to the police station."

NOVEMBER 1906. "One of the white marble bases for the pillars on each side of the main entrance to the Colt Memorial School arrived yesterday afternoon. The massive piece of marble weighs seven tons, and was moved into position this morning by means of blocking and tackles. The derricks, which are capable of lifting four tons, could not be utilized. The slab and its mate will be the heaviest pieces used in the building. It required four horses to haul the slab from Providence."

NOTES

CHAPTER TWO

1. According to a circa 1887 map in the Bristol Town Clerk's office, the streets originally named High, Hope and Thames are still called by those names today; however, Thames Street was sometimes unofficially called Water Street. Other street names have changed over the years; Charles Street, named in honor of King Charles, was changed to King Street, and changed again to the current State Street, but it was also known colloquially as Pump Lane; and Queen Street is now Constitution Street. The list goes on: Jail Lane is Court Street; Taylor's Lane is John Street; Cross Lane is now Milk Street; and Bradford Street was once known as Broad Street. Franklin Street was once part of the L-shaped road that is now Wood Street. In 1942, Charles O.F. Thompson wrote, "Wood Street commences at the foot of Bay View Avenue formerly known as Crooked Lane and ends at Walker's Corner." Metacom Avenue when laid out was Back Road; Mount Hope Avenue was formerly called Mount Lane; and the former Malt-House Lane is now Gooding Avenue.

2. Richard V. Simpson, *Bristol: Montaup to Poppasquash* (Charleston, SC: Arcadia Publishing, 2002), 137–48.

CHAPTER THREE

3. Charles Frederick Jr. (1839–1917) married his fist wife, Mary Potter (1823–1866) of Providence, in 1863. They had one daughter, Julia (1864–1942). He married his second wife, Alice Almy (1838–1931), in 1868.

CHAPTER FIVE

4. Now Chestnut Street.

5. Richard V. Simpson, *Building the Mosquito Fleet: The U.S. Navy's First Torpedo Boats* (Charleston, SC: Arcadia Publishing, 2001).

Notes to Pages 71–137

Chapter Seven

6. Richard V. Simpson, *Bristol, Rhode Island: In the Mount Hope Lands of King Philip* (1996) and *Bristol, Rhode Island: The Bristol Renaissance* (1998).

7. *In the Mount Hope Lands of King Philip* (1996), 477; *The Bristol Renaissance* (1998), 11.

Chapter Nine

8. All of the articles and reports cited in this chapter are available for reference at the Bristol Town Clerk's office.

Chapter Ten

9. The three-story Hasbrouck Building, built in 1896, was reduced to two stories after a disastrous fire on January 7, 1929. Among various retail businesses housed in this building were a motion picture theater and a bowling alley.

Chapter Eleven

10 .This Cianci tale is taken from state and local newspaper accounts, official Fourth of July Committee minutes and personal observations.

11. At the time, Cianci was mayor of the city of Providence, but he was running for governor at the same time. He was allowed to march in the Fourth of July parade as incumbent mayor, but not as a candidate for higher office.

12. *Providence Journal* political reporter M. Charles Bakst, in referring to Cianci, quoted John Randolph (1773–1833): "He is a man of splendid abilities, but utterly corrupt. He shines and stinks like rotten mackerel by moonlight."

13. As a footnote to this tale, it is worth recording that the Rhode Island clambake, as we know it, was invented in 1825 by a Bristolian, even though the site of the momentous occasion was Rocky Point on the west shore of Narragansett Bay. "Invented" may not be the correct word; "reinvented" is more to the truth. The original inhabitants of these shores steamed their food in pits filled with hot rocks and covered with seaweed.

Bibliography

250th Anniversary Committee. *The Book of Bristol.* Bristol, RI: Bristol Phoenix Publishing Co., 1930.

Bacon, Edgar Mayhew. *Narragansett Bay*. New York: The Knickerbocker Press, 1904.

Bowen, Richard LeBaron. *Early Rehoboth, Volume III.* Rehoboth, MA: privately printed, 1948.

Bristol Phoenix, 1850 through 2006, selected issues.

Brownell, Henrietta M.K. *God's Way Man's Way*. New York: The Catholic Publication Society, 1885.

Castro, Raymond. *History of Defiance Hose Co., No. 1, Bristol, RI, 1905–2005*. Bristol, RI: privately printed, 2006.

Clauson, J. Earl. *These Plantations*. Providence, RI: Roger Williams Press, 1937.

Edelstein, Eleanor Rockwell. *A Casual History of Point Pleasant Farm*. Los Angeles: privately printed, 1963.

Federal Writers' Project. *Rhode Island, Guide to the Smallest State*. Boston: Houghton Mifflin Co., 1937.

Field, Edward. *State of Rhode Island and Providence Plantations at the End of the Century: A History*. Boston: The Mason Publishing Co., 1902.

Green, Welcome Arnold. *The Providence Plantations for 250 Years*. Providence, RI: J.A. & R.A. Reid, 1886.

Greene, George Washington. *A Short History of Rhode Island.* Providence, RI: J.A. & R.A. Reid, 1877.

Haley, John Williams. *Mount Hope, A Radio Address.* May 29, 1946.

"The Houses of Bristol, Rhode Island—Part I." *Pencil Points,* June 1936.

"The Houses of Bristol, Rhode Island—Part II." *Pencil Points,* August 1936.

Munro, W.H. *Picturesque Rhode Island.* Providence, RI: J.A. & R.A. Reid, 1881.

———. *The Story of the Mount Hope Lands.* Providence, RI: J.A. & R.A. Reid, 1881.

The Old Stone Bank History of Rhode Island, Vol. III. Providence, RI: Providence Institutions for Savings, 1936.

Preston, Howard Willis. *Rhode Island, and the Sea.* Office of Secretary of State, 1932.

Rhode Island Historical Preservation Commission. *Historic and Architectural Resources of Bristol, Rhode Island.* 1990.

Schultz, Eric B., and Michael J. Tougias. *King Philip's War.* Woodstock, VT: The Countryman Press, 1999.

Thompson, Charles O.F. *Sketches of Old Bristol.* Providence, RI: Roger Williams Press, 1942.

Weeks, Alvin G. *Massasoit of the Wampanoags.* Privately Printed, 1920.

About the Author

I'll be here, waiting and watching for you.

Rhode Island native Richard V. Simpson moved to Bristol in 1961. But his love for the old town began about two decades earlier. He recalls in the mid-1940s, when on most summer and autumn Sunday afternoons his father would pack the family into the Studebaker, and they were off to explore the bucolic plantations of Rhode Island. When not exploring the fields and forests of Arcadia, Hope Valley or Knightsville while bouncing along rutted and worn rural roads, their jaunts most often took them along the shore roads of seaside towns on both sides of Narragansett Bay.

Shortly after coming to Bristol and settling down in an 1810 Federal-style house on High Street, memories of those long-ago Sunday afternoon rides down Bristol's Hope Street came flooding back into Simpson's consciousness: the street shaded by a towering canopy of elm, with elevated sidewalks along an entire block of impressive mansions, commercial and public buildings, the huge Tudor-style YMCA and the impressive red brick Renaissance Revival post office. However, the most unforgettable of those childhood memories was the sight of dozens of gigantic sailboats up on davits, sheltered with canvas covers, giving to each of the craft the look of some hulking prehistoric monster.

Richard's deep-seated interest in the history of the state of Rhode Island now takes a back seat to a greater interest in the history of the town of Bristol. Of his fifteen published nonfiction books, twelve deal with the town of Bristol from its historic beginnings to its contemporary resurgence as a tourist destination. Reasoning that a future generation of Bristol citizens may be curious about the genesis of the East Bay Bike Path that has its beginning/end at Independence Park, and the reason for the town charter form of government, Richard wrote a timeline history of the subjects in his *Bristol: Montaup to Poppasquash* (2002).

Many old-time Bristol-born townies think of nouveau residents like Richard as "carpetbaggers." Regardless of the number of years the "outsider" has lived within the town's boundaries, he or she is forever tagged with this term. Regardless of certain feelings of town-born citizens, Richard says he is comfortable here and has plans of putting down everlasting roots.

Other Books by Richard V. Simpson

Crown of Gold: A History of the Italian-Roman Catholic Church in Bristol, RI (1967)
Independence Day: How the Day is Celebrated in Bristol, RI (1989)
Old St. Mary's: Mother Church in Bristol, RI (1994)
Bristol, Rhode Island: In the Mount Hope Lands of King Philip (1996)
Bristol, Rhode Island: The Bristol Renaissance (1998)
America's Cup Yachts: The Rhode Island Connection (1999)
Building the Mosquito Fleet: U.S. Navy's First Torpedo Boats (2001)
Bristol: Montaup to Poppasquash (2002)
Bristol, Rhode Island: A Postcard History (2005)
Narragansett Bay: A Postcard History (2005)
Herreshoff Yachts: Seven Generations of Industrials, Inventors and Ingenuity in Bristol (2007)

Books by Richard V. Simpson and Nancy J. Devin

Portsmouth, Rhode Island: Pocasset: Ancestral Lands of the Narragansett (1997)
Tiverton and Little Compton, RI: Pocasset and Sakonnet, Wampanoag Country (1997)
Tiverton and Little Compton, Rhode Island: Volume II (1998)